"The most effective and inspiring leaders all have one thing in common. They never forget that they aren't really leading a company, project, or mission; they're leading the people on whom the success of the company, project, or mission actually depends. In *The Human Team*, we're delightfully and powerfully reminded that, just as individual humans have universal needs that must be met to reach self-actualization, human teams have requirements for reaching their full potential. Using a blend of relatable stories and case studies with scientific reference points, this book gives a clear framework for understanding and meeting those needs to create healthy teams and healthy bottom lines."

Dixie Gillaspie, business coach, firestarter, and author of *Just Blow It Up: Firepower for Living an Unlimited Life*

"Adaptability and optimization are keys to the future of work and success. Coaching their people and teams on the 6 Facets of Human Needs will help every leader leverage humanity and focus the right energy by nurturing their teams to achieve the next level of success in business."

Jonathan B. Smith, founder, Optimize for Growth

"As somebody who doesn't love the 'people stuff,' I've learned the hard way that leading a team is so much more than just getting the right people doing the right things. In *The*

Human Team, Jeanet has totally nailed the missing link between nature and nurture. And what I love most is that she's provided solid science and instantly actionable steps to turn your leadership into a real asset!"

Josh Turner, founder, LinkedSelling and Connect 365

"Packed with updated science and real stories of struggle and triumph, this book will especially appeal to leaders of entrepreneurial companies because of its practical applications to our everyday lives! We can no longer assume that humans are getting their needs met at home or in their social groups. Jeanet calls on all leaders to step up and be champions of making sure the needs of the human team are met. She does it with grace, wit, and approachability, sharing her vivid stories freely so that we may learn from them."

Jill Young, author of the *Advantage Series for Entrepreneurial Leadership Teams*

"I have worked with Jeanet as a colleague and friend, sharing client companies over the years, as we strive to develop leaders. I admire Jeanet and how she can guide organizations by simplifying their approach to leading a business. In *The Human Team*, she shares her special 'secret sauce' by embracing her own humanness and treating others like humans as well. I would encourage leaders to get Jeanet's book and use it as a guide to explore the human teams around us."

Jonathan Jones, master chair, CEO coach, peer group facilitator, Vistage Worldwide—St. Louis

THE HUMAN
TEAM

JEANET WADE

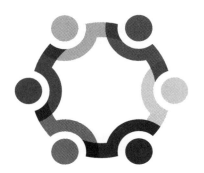

THE HUMAN TEAM

SO, YOU CREATED A TEAM BUT PEOPLE SHOWED UP!

ForbesBooks

Published by ForbesBooks, Charleston, South Carolina.
Member of Advantage Media Group.

ForbesBooks is a registered trademark, and the ForbesBooks colophon is a trademark of Forbes Media, LLC.

Printed in the United States of America.

10 9 8 7 6 5 4 3 2 1

ISBN: 978-1-95086-332-7
LCCN: 2020922359

Cover design by David Taylor.
Layout design by Carly Blake.

This custom publication is intended to provide accurate information and the opinions of the author in regard to the subject matter covered. It is sold with the understanding that the publisher, Advantage|ForbesBooks, is not engaged in rendering legal, financial, or professional services of any kind. If legal advice or other expert assistance is required, the reader is advised to seek the services of a competent professional.

Advantage Media Group is proud to be a part of the Tree Neutral® program. Tree Neutral offsets the number of trees consumed in the production and printing of this book by taking proactive steps such as planting trees in direct proportion to the number of trees used to print books. To learn more about Tree Neutral, please visit **www.treeneutral.com**.

Since 1917, Forbes has remained steadfast in its mission to serve as the defining voice of entrepreneurial capitalism. ForbesBooks, launched in 2016 through a partnership with Advantage Media Group, furthers that aim by helping business and thought leaders bring their stories, passion, and knowledge to the forefront in custom books. Opinions expressed by ForbesBooks authors are their own. To be considered for publication, please visit **www.forbesbooks.com**.

To Marshall:
Thank you for allowing me to have "human moments"
and loving me when my "human happens."
I've learned and grown from your support, love, and
encouragement. This book—and many other things—
wouldn't be possible if you were not in my life.

CONTENTS

INTRODUCTION

O ver the past few decades, I've seen leaders, managers, and facilitators succeed, and I've seen them fail. The common denominator in both cases? People! Let's face it: we're all in the people business. People tend to be our greatest sense of accomplishment—and our greatest frustration.

Some of you are reading this book to help solve common frustrations: ineffective people, inability to sustain engagement, worry over tough people decisions, or just feeling that managing people is not your favorite part of the job. Others are reading to learn to continue to improve the workplace environment and invest in the power of people in order to leverage "return on individuals."

I've always had a passion for understanding people and team dynamics, and over the course of my career, I've discovered how to harness human energy out of "human moments." I've helped individuals, teams, and organizations to improve their overall health, retention, engagement, loyalty, motivation, adaptability, and financial results. I wrote this book to share these insights and help you crack the code to cultivating human energy and unleashing stronger outcomes for your people, teams, and organizations.

I was recently reminded by an NPR *TED Radio Hour* that *innovation* comes from sampling and borrowing in order to create new concepts, ideas, and frameworks. This is a good part of what I have done in my work as a team leader, consultant, and coach. This book is both a culmination of that work and a guidebook to move you more efficiently, effectively, and joyfully along your own path of leading the people on your teams. It can help you to shift some of what you already know about business and working with people, bringing you deeper levels of awareness about the human beings on your team and guiding you through the best practices I've developed to nurture and engage them. Ultimately, this journey is about bridging the nature/ nurture gap, addressing the needs that are rooted in human nature, so you can nurture your people to excellence.

For part of my research and development into the concepts on which I base my work, I enlisted the help of Dr. Patricia Bagsby. You'll find her academic and scientific expertise interspersed throughout the book in the highlighted sections titled "Dr. Tricia's Take." As an expert in organizational and leadership development, she's consulted for numerous businesses and helped them achieve substantial people-fueled results. I'm confident her insights will be as helpful to you as they are for me.

Writing this book has been a personal and professional journey for me, and in it I share my experiences. In each of the core chapters, I've included a personal vignette that testifies to the importance of specific human needs at work. I hope that the sometimes vulnerable moments that I've shared on my path to becoming a business leader can serve as sources of inspiration (or cautionary tales).

The stories I've included are also there to make an even greater, more central point—successful people are just human, on a journey of self-improvement. As you'll discover, my entrepreneurial and leadership journey has been one of "progress not perfection." Every challenge contains an opportunity, and the quest we're all on is to take each challenge and fully employ the opportunity it offers. Thank you for letting me, through this book, be part of your quest to be an empowered and empowering leader.

Now, let's begin your journey to understanding your Human Team!

SIX
FACETS
of
HUMAN
NEEDS

CONFIDENCE
CLARITY
CONNECTION
CONTRIBUTION
CHALLENGE
CONSIDERATION

CHAPTER 1

From Experience and Observation—
Six Facets of Human Needs

*"The most exciting breakthrough of the 21st century
will occur not because of technology, but because of an
expanding concept of what it means to be human."*

—JOHN NAISBITT, *MEGATRENDS*

was asked to do a presentation on team health for an annual conference for business leaders. I asked the event organizer why I had
been tapped for that track and was told, "I asked around, and
everyone agreed that you're known for really understanding how to
create healthy teams, how to really facilitate people's energy to the
best outcome for all, and for having worked with a wide variety of
teams successfully."

When I thought about it, I realized it was true. Not only was I
passionate about team health, individual adaptability, and productiv-

ity, but I also had experienced and observed humanity while working in the incentive and motivation industry while tapping into human behavior as a marketing leader and while helping business owners and managers solve their people challenges.

As I began to reflect on my over twenty-five years in business, including more than five hundred full days with leadership teams as a business coach helping them navigate to healthy outcomes, I began to make detailed notes about the times I had succeeded and times when I was challenged and the times when I had seen people and/or teams succeed.

As I compiled and analyzed my notes, it became more and more clear to me that the successes I had seen were predicated on times when certain needs were met for individuals, teams, and organizations. And in each of the case studies where there were far less than stellar outcomes or outright crash-and-burn failures, I could easily identify one or more basic human needs that were not met, causing the team to develop an unhealthy or toxic dynamic.

Put more simply, I realized that, much like any growing thing, if people are working in an environment that doesn't provide their basic needs as a human being, no amount of nurturing is going to result in a productive outcome. Think of the sunflower, for instance. If it is planted in the shade or in a bog, no amount of fertilizer or other nurturing encouragement will result in a healthy plant, much less a crop of seeds. Nature certainly needs nurture. But providing for needs must precede nurturing for there to be a return on that investment.

Those realizations put me on a path, my own personal quest, for a deeper understanding of what all humans need to thrive and prosper or even to respond to nurturing when it is provided. That path led me here, to sharing with you the 6 Facets of Human Needs™, or what I call "the 6 Cs."

I want to share with you some personal stories that really high-lighted the truth of this work for me. As I've said, every challenge comes with an opportunity, and these were some of my earliest and most difficult challenges. They were also some of the greatest learning and growth opportunities my career has offered to date, and without examining them frankly and with compassion for myself and everyone involved I would not be the leader I am today, and this book would not exist.

WHEN TOXICITY IMPACTS A TEAM

I was midpoint in my career when I encountered an office bully and was on a leadership team in a toxic work environment where the negative side of human nature flourished and there was no focus on team health.

I began this executive leadership opportunity with confidence, armed with over a decade of experience in growing organizations just like this. Since I'd been involved on the ground floor, I understood and had helped develop the company's mission. Our team was virtual, and because we were all connected to the main leader but not to one other, we quickly became dysfunctional—even toxic. Large competing egos began working at cross-purposes. A lack of communication yielded to (at times) aggressive communication and open conflict.

An example of this happened during an off-site executive meeting when a bully on the leadership team raised a seemingly trivial topic: business cards. As head of marketing, product development, sales, and customer service, I had taken lead on the cards and asked one of my graphic designers to create an original corporate design. As anyone with printing experience understands, you never reorder cards from designers because they'll upcharge you. But to my amazement, the bully had unilaterally reached out to my graphic designer and, instead of contacting a printer, ordered the business cards from her. And the invoice we received was predictably expensive.

In the midst of discussing high-level strategy, launching major initiatives, targeting new markets, and identifying long-term growth objectives, the bully broached the topic of business cards and derailed the entire meeting:

"This graphic designer is charging us *triple* the usual costs of business cards," she announced. "This is *your* contact, Jeanet, and firmly in your area. Why do you bring these kinds of people into our organization?"

Shocked by the comment, I froze, while the rest of the group responded with indignation. This had to be resolved, they all agreed, and if this type of behavior persisted, the board would shame us for such flagrant overspending. Suddenly, I was cast as the culprit for fiscal mismanagement. All because of overpriced business cards that I had never ordered in the first place!

I fixed the financial problem with my graphic designer, with whom I had a solid professional rapport, but my relationship with the executive team never recovered.

Following that meeting the toxicity seeped into the very fabric of the organization and infected my relationships with others. The bully instigated back-channel politicking and gave false reports on me. But even more painfully, my long-term friend and mentor of almost twenty years was caught in the bully's spell. He'd watched me thrive with multiple projects and clients in many different environments, all the while serving as a close coworker, mentor, boss, colleague, and coach.

One day my mentor, whom I'll call Bill, looked at me and said, "You're not who you used to be."

"You're right," I responded. "And neither are you."

The hostile climate escalated and became scarily unpredictable. One day, my mentor might yell at me on the phone and with colorful language ("What the *&^%, Jeanet!") to describe how inadequate I and my team were. The following day, I might receive a fruit basket with a gift card reading, "You're critical to the team and we value you."

Plagued by self-doubt and an increasing level of organizational distrust, I was unable to engage in healthy disagreement with anyone. That meant that all disagreement, which was rampant in the organization, manifested as undermining and aggressive conflict, with the bully at the epicenter orchestrating events. A feeling of helplessness gradually overcame me, and I mentally checked out of the job.

I couldn't believe it. I'd helped write the business plan and secure funding for this entire venture. I'd created the logos, forged the brand, and helped assemble the team. But within the span of six months, I'd devolved into complete ineffectiveness. I gained weight and became sick multiple times in a row. For my own sanity, I eventually had to leave.

If we had focused on team health, we could have achieved great things.

As always, hindsight offers its own perspectives. Knowing what I know now about team health and human needs, I can see that the leadership team and the organization failed because of an inability to understand the dysfunctional human nature dynamics, like self-protection, and not meeting the needs of the people or the team. If we had focused on team health, we could have achieved great things.

This harrowing situation was a low point in my diverse career as an employee, employer, team leader, and business coach. This experience was the catalyst for a deeper dive into understanding team dynamics.

A DIVERSITY OF TEAMS

I've had a diverse career in which I've always leveraged humanity and the dynamics of people on teams. The following experiences are where I gathered the information, learnings, and observations that led to my discovery of human needs on teams.

I began my career in the 1990s, at a St. Louis–based motivation and incentive company. Situated in a large organization, my team focused on innovation. And, true to its purpose, it was *actually innovative*. My organizational division invented the world's very first gift card. I was junior in my career, but I'd helped launch and create the communications materials and websites to support the card, along with other related products and initiatives.

Anyone who worked for this organization was well trained in Maslow's hierarchy of needs. And that piqued my interest because a few years prior to joining the company, I'd met my future husband. A keen self-discovery enthusiast, he introduced me to the world of self-improvement literature. This meant that, at this early and formative juncture of my career, while beginning my work in the motivation and incentive industry, I embarked on my own quest for self-improvement and self-actualization, devouring anything from Tony Robbins to clinical scholarship in the field.

The culture of the organization emphasized freedom and autonomy, and in this environment of healthy challenge, I thrived. My professional relationships were positive, and I was successful, accumulating promotions, appreciation awards, and other incentives. Absorbing the positive energy of this work environment, I leaned into my self-discovery journey and signed up for educational opportunities in management, Maslow's hierarchy of needs, and the organization's mission. Seeking to hone my specialty, I even devoured an audiotape series on incentives and motivation.

When that division of the company merged to become a joint venture with American Express, I continued on, assuming the role of web business development.

In this role I had to run interference among rival teams claiming the digital space, all the while meeting with boards of directors to convince them that this newfangled thing called the internet was important. It was my first experience in leading teams, and it was dizzying. We launched fourteen different types of website initiatives within three or four months and developed a series of applications for creating incentive programs. This was a time when launching websites was a major undertaking. Getting those teams to advance during this moment of change was a fascinating challenge. Sometimes I relinquished control entirely, letting them operate autonomously, and sometimes I'd provide bite-size bits of strategy instead of overwhelming them with the big picture. It was early in my career, and I was experimenting with my leadership style. I didn't it know it then, but upon reflection I was helping the team contribute effectively, challenging them when needed and instilling confidence to create new capabilities.

In 2000 I left this stable and fulfilling opportunity to work for a large broadband start-up, and I was head of strategy for one of its subsidiaries. While I'd participated in an official start-up before, it existed under the umbrella of a large corporation. Now I was in a legitimate start-up—you know, the kind that relies on venture backing and notoriously lacks clarity and direction.

Our initial investors had allowed the company to hire very quickly, and so we began with seventy-five to one hundred people. But because of this hiring frenzy, we were thrown together haphazardly. You guessed it: we had a marked lack of clarity and structure. While I'd always thrived on challenge, I was ill prepared for tackling one in which a hundred people had no idea about their roles and purposes in the larger organizational mission. I didn't realize it at the time, but unlike the role I had just left, this was an environment where my human needs weren't met and where the team was constantly in self-preservation mode, an instinct that leads to big egos and difficult social dynamics.

Thinking about my strengths in gathering teams to deliver outcomes, especially in the fields of marketing and strategy, I then decided to start my own business and launched Jalapeno Marketing and Consulting.

It's been a long road of credentialing, practice, and trial and error to arrive at where I am now, one of the top business strategists and coaches in my region. My early career in the incentives and motivation industry provided a great foundation, as it helped me to understand people—what makes them tick and what incents them to modify their behaviors to reach goals and achieve results.

My work in marketing, which has spanned several decades, has also helped considerably. While participating in marketing campaigns, I posed the same questions about human behavior but in a different context, trying to meet a human need or truth in a product or service campaign with compelling, high-impact messaging.

My experience in marketing has taught me that it's the human element that creates success. Remember the Got Milk? campaign? It's decades old, but you still probably remember little children and celebrities donning milk mustaches with the tag line Got Milk? nearby. That encapsulates everything you need in a successful campaign: short, crisp, and clear messaging that addresses a human truth. We've all had the experience of needing to balance something sweet with something savory—we just all understand that intuitively. And because it resonated with this human truth, we went out and purchased milk—

even if the research was unclear about whether it was actually good for us. Nike's Just Do It campaign achieved something similar, addressing, in a pithy and compelling way, the powerful human need to move our bodies in confidence.

For me, marketing was always about making a branding campaign resonate on a psychic, human level. Before embarking on each campaign, I've always asked, "What need does this address in our target audience?" I took that spirit to a DC area construction company, specializing in doing upgrades and enhancements for publicly funded facilities for local government, military, and school campuses. As lead of the outsourced marketing team, I started by finding out the key frustrations or motivations of my client's clients—facility managers. Such a business-to-business operation can't use a business-to-consumer advertising technique like "Got Milk?" and "Just Do It" but still had to respond to a human need. My preliminary research revealed that the vast majority of these facility managers were under considerable pressure to finish projects and were burdened with a seemingly endless list of backlogged projects.

To tap into their human truth, we scratched some of the predictable marketing materials like booths, glossy brochures, and banners advertising construction services. Instead, we hired a group of massage therapists at an industry event that read, "Relax the Backlog." That's right: instead of promoting our services, we advertised back rubs! While we had this captive audience, receiving their self-care, we told them that if they needed to relax their construction backlog as well, we had some services for that too. If they were interested, they received little handouts, in the form of little mints in a prescription bottle, to keep them on theme for temporary relief from Construction Backlog Stress Disorder. "Please contact us today to schedule a visit with our professional and find a cure," the bottle read. The campaign was as effective as it was profitable. Though the numbers fluctuated, the CFO announced that our marketing efforts over five years translated into a 300 percent increase in revenues.

Beginning around 2013, I pivoted again to helping leadership teams of privately held companies execute their strategic vision with healthy teams. This involves solidifying and aligning strategy so that everyone is accountable and teams are cohesive, ultimately able to achieve their larger visions. To this end, as a Business Alchemist (my current company), I facilitate full-day off-site meetings with leadership teams at privately held companies. As I write this book, I've conducted over five hundred sessions and counting. In this Business Laboratory (my term for these off-site sessions), I facilitate, teach, and coach leadership teams so they can make their organizations stronger. In these five-hundred-plus off-sites, it's just me and three to seven people, addressing human needs and human nature to achieve business results. Just as in incentives and motivation and marketing, it's the same struggle: dealing with people.

MY SECRET SAUCE TO TEAM HEALTH: THE 6 FACETS OF HUMAN NEEDS (6 Cs)

Throughout my twenty-five years serving on project, department, and leadership teams and two decades spent in marketing, I came to understand the underlying dynamics governing team thriving, stagnation and unfulfillment, and unfortunate lapses into complacency and toxicity. But it was only in the last eight years observing clients in my Business Laboratory that my thinking about human nature and needs crystallized and even became more scientific and quantitative. With the wealth of observation, experience, and repetition in these five hundred full-day sessions, I discovered that success and failure largely hinge on 6 Facets of Human Needs. These are my "6 Cs," the subject of this book.

Clarity is the first major facet. Think of clarity as focus and direction—the opposite of confusion. A lack of clarity among team members also leads to lack of *connection*, the second ingredient to my secret sauce of thriving teams. You can think of connection as belonging and integration in a social environment at work.

When people lack clarity about roles and expectations and/or don't feel like they have a legitimate place on the team, chances are they will not be willing or able to contribute, which is the third need I identified. *Contribution* is so important because it's connected to purpose and meaning, among the highest of human aspirations.

When people have clarity and connection and they are making contributions to the team, they are ready for healthy challenges, the fourth of the 6 Cs. Human beings thrive when ensconced in atmospheres of healthy *challenge*. At a recent off-site meeting, I was reminded of this again when a participant approached me and said, "I want to thank you for challenging me and pushing me to accomplish these things and make me better than I ever thought I could be."

This feedback was gratifying because it reminded me of how fulfilling healthy challenges can be—they can help us activate latent potentials and ascend Maslow's famous hierarchy of needs to achieve the pinnacle of self-actualization. Challenge is a means of continuous improvement that leads to mastery. Challenge is the metaphorical pressure that transforms carbon into diamonds. Challenge is also at the heart of innovation.

But in order to be challenged in productive and meaningful ways, human beings must be afforded *consideration*, facet number five. You can think of consideration as appreciation, respect, and value. Consideration is nothing less than the recognition of mutual humanity.

And with our humanity acknowledged and respected, we create

room for my final facet of human need: *confidence.* Confidence means courage and bravery. If I'm confident in my abilities, I'm courageous enough to solicit feedback and metabolize constructive criticism because I'm always seeking to improve.

Of course, there are examples of missing all the facets of human needs in my examples of the toxic environments I experienced, and I'll be referring to them throughout the book. But these stories serve to illustrate how missing any of these facets lead to fear, apprehension, and doubt and can quash confidence. Without confidence, you can't commit to your own self-improvement, let alone to the objectives of a team or the mission of an organization. This final facet is most aligned to Maslow's sixth and final human need, of self-actualization. If I'm self-actualized, I can stand in a place of confidence.

During my current work in coaching leadership and executive teams, and throughout my diverse career experiences, I've found these 6 Facets of Human Needs to be essential. When they are fully accounted for in our teams, we're able to gel with one another, operate harmoniously, engage in healthy disagreement, and achieve important objectives. As leaders, managers, and project facilitators, we've all been on such teams, and we've all hired people who seem to manifest and even radiate these six key qualities. Such people are easy to manage and a pleasure to work with.

Unfortunately, we also know that the opposite is far more common. Oftentimes, we get frustrated by people on our teams who don't seem to fit. We respond by throwing leadership development, engagement workshops, and teamwork exercises their way. This isn't a bad idea. In fact, sometimes such interventions result in a momentary sense of connection and even a collective high. But these positive outcomes inevitably prove short term. The underlying problem, I argue in this book, is that most of us don't realize we're missing one of these six vital facets of human need—the 6 Cs. A teams' success or failure hinges on the presence or absence of these six facets.

And yet, as the personal experiences I've already shared and the variety of client stories I've included in future chapters clearly illustrate, when these needs are met, many of the common frustrations that plague leaders and managers begin to go away, leading to increased congruence, collaboration, adaptability, and yes, profitability.

You can think of my 6 Facets of Human Needs (6 Cs) as Maslow's hierarchy of needs geared toward teams instead of individuals. When doing individual self-improvement, Maslow remains an industry gold standard. But when focusing on the unique needs of people when functioning in teams, we need the 6 Cs: *connection* to ourselves and others, *confidence* in our teammates, the ability to positively *contribute*, *clarity* about our roles, healthy *challenges* to elicit our professional best, and *consideration* from others.

This book outlines the 6 Facets of Human Needs (6 Cs) in detail. I devote each chapter to one facet of this framework, showing how you can bridge the nature/nurture gap and operationalize these principles. But before we can explore these 6 Cs in detail, we need to ground ourselves in human nature. What sets my framework apart is that it prioritizes human nature prior to introducing nurture-based interventions. We now turn to a discussion of topics like brain chemistry and human instinct—the core parts of human nature that are vital to understand in our workplaces. It's only after we unpack the physiological dynamics unwittingly governing organizational team dynamics that we can begin to harness them in productive ways.

A note to you, the leader, manager, or facilitator of people:

Through this journey you will gain clarity on how to build connection with the people on your teams, allowing them to fully contribute and for you to challenge them to greater outcomes. Please be considerate of those on your teams and apply the concepts in this book so that you and your teams reach new levels of confidence.

With that, I challenge you to read one chapter per day and reflect on how you can apply the concepts and framework to individuals that you coach and teams that you lead. By doing so you will see that the people that "showed up" with their human nature can be nurtured to greater outcomes once you've met the needs of your Human Team.

CHAPTER 2

Human Happens

"Leadership is all about people. It is not about organizations. It is not about plans. It is not about strategies. It is all about people—motivating people to get the job done. You have to be people-centered."

—COLIN POWELL

t's a tale as old as time. You hire a new person to your company or assign someone new to one of your teams. The person strikes you as promising for the role, and you're optimistic. Day one arrives, and the new hire / team member is nervous but excited, infused with promise and possibility and poised to contribute to a new goal or organizational mission. Everything starts off great—maybe a few hiccups here and there but nothing terrible. Then, gradually and sometimes inevitably, enthusiasm diminishes; engagement declines. Most leaders respond to this predicament as follows: "This would have worked out well if it weren't for this person."

Admit it: when teams break down and when employees disengage, leaders and managers typically don't question their strategies and instead assign blame to the people appointed to carry them out. When charitable, leaders and managers cast such people as bad fits, and at their worst, they call them whiners, complainers, or failures. But this is wrong. In about 80 percent of cases, I believe that the people aren't defective at all. Most such situations represent a failure of our leaders to understand and address human nature.

Team health is predicated on understanding and harnessing human nature. Unfortunately, most leaders begin with nurture, leveraging well-meaning leadership tools like motivation and teamwork exercises and soft skills training initiatives. Such leadership interventions represent a quick dose of medicine—a Band-Aid on a bleeding wound, or a duct tape and twine solution to quickly fix a broken slat on a staircase. They feel great and might give your team a quick adrenaline boost (or at least prevent a swollen ankle). The effects are short-lived, mostly because they come out of sequence. We must first address human nature before we can nurture our teams into greater outcomes. I formulated the 6 Facets of Human Needs (6 Cs) to bridge the gap from nature to nurture. If you start with human nature and human needs, you'll find that your job as a leader, manager, and coach becomes easier as your teams are primed to receive effective nurturing.

"How humans work is how they work at work."

—JEANET WADE

HUMAN BEINGS ARE FASCINATING!

Bridging the Gap between Nature and Nurture

NEEDS
- Clarity
- Connection
- Contribution
- Challenge
- Consideration
- Confidence

NATURE
- Instincts
- MO
- Brain Function

NURTURE
- Engagement
- Coaching
- Motivation

THE BEGUILING BRAIN

The first vital component of human nature is brain function. Fundamentally, and too simply, brain function concerns the amygdala. When human beings encounter something stressful—the proverbial lion on the savanna, a close call on the freeway, conflict with a spouse or coworker—the brain's amygdala, responsible for a host of functions like fear, sadness, memory, and aggression, sends danger signals to our brain's command center, the hypothalamus. The hypothalamus, in turn, disseminates the news to the rest of the nervous system, resulting in sweaty palms, a pounding heart, and difficult breathing.[1] We've all been there. This suite of reactions was once termed "fight or flight," but modern specialists, using contemporary science, have updated it to "freeze, flee, fight."[2]

Oftentimes at work, we trip our brain's fight/flight/freeze cascade and we're baffled by the reactions. We don't know why some aggressively lash out or freeze. According to Joseph LeDoux, a professor of science at New York University and director of the Emotional Brain Institute, that's understandable.

"Freezing is not a choice," he observes. "It is a built-in impulse controlled by ancient circuits in the brain involving the amygdala and its neural partners and is automatically set into motion by external threats."[3]

Our government agencies are just as unaware of this neuro-chemistry as our workplaces. Consider the FBI and Department of Homeland Security, which suggest that Americans "run, hide, [and] fight" during an active shooter event. The idea underlying this sequence is commonsensical enough: flee the scene if possible, hide if you can't, and, as a last resort, attempt a struggle with the gun-wielding lunatic.[4] But as Professor LeDoux says, commenting on this protocol, "Underlying the idea of 'run, hide, fight' is the presumption that volitional choices are readily available in situations of danger. But the fact is, when you are in danger, whether it is a bicyclist speeding at you or a shooter locked and loaded, you may well find yourself frozen, unable to act and think clearly."[5]

As we've learned from past active shooter tragedies, some of us naturally fall into a fight, flight, or freeze mode. We've learned the same in our workplaces. As leaders and managers, we don't always recognize the brain function behind employee disengagement or other unfortunate behaviors like incessant complaining. As Professor LeDoux understands, in order to get to a more reasoned "run, hide, fight" stance—instead of just reacting—we must work at it and activate less primitive parts of the brain (like creating new pathways in our neocortex).[6] To outsmart our primitive brains in a work setting, we need to focus on the 6 Cs. When these fundamental facets of human needs and fulfillment are met, we're less likely to trip our primitive neural reactions.

At a recent leadership event, the facilitator described a study that astonished the group. Me included. As one hundred study participants were advised, something negative was going to happen to them. And it did: a female pickpocketed them. To avoid ethical complications, the participants were immediately reunited with their property, assured of their personal safety, and then interviewed about what had occurred. To the horror of the audience, each nearly described the same thing: they were bodychecked or physically assaulted by a physically strong, large male, usually wearing a hoodie. (Had it been a hundred years ago, the researchers surmised, it would have been a trench coat.)

Brain chemistry was at fault. The amygdalae of these "victims" were activated, fight/flight/freeze chemicals surged throughout their bodies, and memory formation and recall were compromised (to say the least!). Instead of reliable recall, these brains pulled from preexisting memories, like scripts of movies, past experiences, books, and news stories. Study participants' brains, in essence, said, "Well if this happened, it must have unfolded like this prior event."

Though this study is scary, showing how fallible our memories are, it shouldn't come as a surprise. We intuitively know that our bodies aren't designed as tape recorders that faithfully capture historical events, especially during moments of trauma. We know the opposite is true: our bodies are designed to sharpen our focus during times of threat, heightening our awareness so we can protect ourselves.[7] Criminal justice reformers and academics have documented this, with some campaigning against the pivotal role of eyewitness testimony, a cornerstone of the American criminal justice system. As of 2011, thousands of studies, undertaken over the span of three decades, had queried the value of eyewitness testimony, many of which demonstrated its inadequacies.[8] According to Brandon L. Garrett, a law professor at the University of Virginia and author of *Convicting the Innocent*, eyewitness testimony has many problems.

"Of the first 250 DNA exonerations," for example, "190 involved eyewitnesses who were wrong."[9] The results can ruin human lives, cost untold damage to our tax base (paying monumental restitution awards for wrongful conviction), and plague our workplaces.

> **Bottom line: As a leader or manager, please remember that there are diverse perspectives on the truth at work on your teams.**

Bottom line: As a leader or manager, please remember that there are diverse perspectives on the truth at work on your teams. At best these individual perspectives are only about 60 percent accurate when telling a story or recounting events.[10] To begin to address these multiple perspectives on truth, we must create what Harvard Business School professor Amy Edmondson called "psychological safety" in our workplaces.[11] Our workplaces must allow for us to safely share our perspectives and safely disagree ("I see things slightly differently than you, as I believe X"). From such a baseline of human consideration, we can begin to overcome our brain's built-in defenses and start to arrive at a common perspective. As a bonus, we'll do better. As decades of Professor Edmondson's research has revealed, trusting companies are better performing ones.[12]

FATAL INSTINCT

Working from a common perspective could have helped me overcome an instinctual reaction I inadvertently triggered during an executive off-site meeting. Six months into working for a start-up—the same start-up that contained the bully I described in chapter 1—the executive group broached the topic of bonuses. It's common wisdom that smart start-ups don't award bonuses. In fact, many leaders endure modest salaries or zero pay, investing time and money into the organization in hopes of a larger future payoff. When I heard rumblings of bonuses, I had the audacity to disagree: "I've worked with a lot of start-ups as a coach and consultant, and this is my second round on a start-up. I've never had anyone talk about bonuses at this stage in the game, especially when we have no product, no income, no active clients. We're not making money. Let's consider tabling this discussion."

The entire team turned on me. I'd unleashed a self-preservation instinct in them. In a primitive sense, I'd threatened their physiological security, the lowest rung of safety on Maslow's hierarchy of needs. They'd all come to the meeting thinking about their financial needs, like mortgage payments, retirement savings, higher education payments for their children, and the like. Because I'd threatened their financial self-preservation, they went into collective "fight" mode.

"Let's take Jeanet down," they seemed to be saying in unison. "She's trying to take our money away!"

Such behavior was a manifestation of human instinct. There are three biological drives or instincts: self-preservation, social acceptance, and sexual. I focus on the first two, and leave other experts, who've written on sexual harassment, the #metoo movement, and related topics, to tackle the last.

Had I been more attuned to the self-preservation instinct, not to mention the tendency for tribes to scapegoat individuals when under threat, I would have reframed self-preservation in the following way:

"College payments and fully funding your 401(k) next month are important, and I understand your concern. But these are short-term financial obligations. If we sacrifice now to create a self-sustaining, solvent, and vibrant organization, we can ensure ourselves a steady stream of bonuses at a later time."

Were I possessed of the foresight to reframe in this way—orienting the group away from individual self-preservation to organizational self-preservation—I could have defused the hostility I endured or even prevented it altogether. In fact, we could have made progress as a team.

Throughout our businesses, physiological instincts are at work in our teams, insidiously affecting our happiness and productivity. I use the word *insidious* because instinctual reactions occur in the background and we don't recognize them until the behavior becomes more obvious—usually more obviously toxic. Instincts stand behind worker disengagement and dissatisfaction rates and stymie the growth and innovative potential of our organizations. People aren't aware they are in a constant state of reaction to physiological stimuli.

DRAMA TRIANGLE

We move around the triangle until one of us moves out and into a healthy communication pattern. Stop the drama!

PERSECUTOR (BULLY) TO CHALLENGER

- Critical
- Pulls others down
- Dominating

RESCUER (SAVIOR) TO COACH

- Feels guilt if not rescuing
- Often expects to fail
- Feels connected when others are dependent

VICTIM (HELPLESS) TO SURVIVOR/THRIVER

- Feels oppressed, hopeless, and ashamed
- Seeks out Rescuer
- Refuses to make decisions

© *Steve Karpman, Karpman Drama Triangle from Transactional Analysis*

When left unchecked, our self-preservation and social acceptance instincts can create a lot of drama in the workplace. When people are out of balance, they begin to seek out one of the personality types identified on this graph: bullies and persecutors, rescuers and saviors, and victims. Heroes, for example, who come in the form of saviors, are deceptively great. The recipients of seemingly well-earned awards and accolades, they are hard to recognize at first because their heroism masks itself as incessant help of others. But their "overhelp" creates codependencies within groups, crippling the development of others. Victims, likewise, might manifest as complainers—the people who complain to you incessantly and constantly seek validation from you or others. To quote business coach and author Steve Chandler, "Needy is creepy." There's nothing more disconcerting and ultimately counterproductive than people who need constant reassurance.[13]

DRAMA ROLES TIED TO HUMAN INSTINCTS

SELF-PROTECTION SPECTRUM
Martyr ◄——— balance ———► Bully

SOCIAL ACCEPTANCE SPECTRUM
Needy ◄——— balance ———► Hero

We all have needy moments, and we all strongly or personally identify with certain projects and initiatives, striving to be something of a hero when working on them. We might even exhibit such tendencies on a macro or generational scale. The Greatest Generation, for example, had a tendency toward heroism. They are justly celebrated for subordinating their own personal needs for the greater good, like defeating Nazism in Europe. Millennials, according to popular stereotype, gravitate to the needy side of the spectrum, seeking recognition and reassurance. When viewed through the prism of human nature, both represent unhealthy and out-of-balance extremes. Absent rebalancing, we'll embrace heroes until they become toxic, stunting the growth of others on the team, and we'll shame the needy until they can't perform.

When it comes to self-preservation, however, the dynamic flips. In a dynamic of social acceptance, we embrace heroes (until they become toxic) and shame the needy, perhaps suggesting they are "entitled millennials" or people who needlessly create drama. But when it comes to organizational self-preservation, we cherish the martyrs and shame the heroes as bullies. Let me explain. We all know the tireless executive assistants: the people who give up their nights and weekends, sacrificing everything for the team and organization. They're martyring themselves and sometimes experience burnout or nervous breakdowns. As heroes, they give until they burn out or lapse into resentment. As I've observed, when it comes to organizational preservation, heroes/bullies are often productive revenue earners like salespeople or organizational visionaries. They might be blunt and difficult interpersonally, but we think of them as keeping our organizations afloat and therefore tolerate their behavior. Bullies/heroes know they are high earners, and that gives them license to bully. Everyone's afraid of them, but no one wants to call them out, even if they know it would be healthier for the organization.

While some of these tendencies are inbred or generational, the 6 Cs help us identify when they become habitual and stymie the productivity of a group. Sadly, our newspapers are full of terrible statistics about bullying in our organizations and schools. By addressing the 6 Cs, as we do in detail throughout this book, we can address the underlying causes—self-preservation (a spectrum of behavior from martyrs to bullies) and social acceptance (a spectrum of behavior from needy to hero)—and then transcend them altogether. In cultivating social acceptance, we can avoid these behavioral extremes and allow our teams to focus on achieving their goals instead.

WHAT'S YOUR MODUS OPERANDI, REALLY?

Like brain function and instinct, people have naturally occurring tendencies that some specialists term modus operandi (MO).

One of the best tools for understanding MOs is a personal assessment called the Kolbe A™ Index. Other popular assessment tools include Wonderlic, Myers-Briggs, and DiSC, which are primarily designed to help us understand the affective (feelings) or cognitive (thinking) parts of our minds, helping us understand how our personalities and emotions influence behavior. The Kolbe A Index, by contrast, zeroes in on the conative part of the brain, which is based on natural instincts and tendencies—therefore human nature.[14] Kolbe is a fabulously insightful and pragmatic tool for teams. Theorist and author Kathy Kolbe spent decades of testing the idea underlying the system: individual ability is dictated by instinct, not personality or intelligence.[15] The Kolbe A Index is the fruit of a decade of work, in which she surveyed and indexed 200,000 people from all over the globe and completed an astonishing 250,000 individual assessments.

All this research and rigorous testing led her to conclude that human instincts cluster into four discernable tendencies: "*Fact Finders* who have the instinct to probe and excel at evaluating and deliberating; *Follow-Thrus* who show the instinct to pattern and thrive when coordinating, planning and scheduling; *Quick-Starts* who have the instinct to innovate and flourish when they originate, experiment and improvise, and *Implementors* who show the instinct to demonstrate by constructing, repairing and crafting."[16] She then created a suite of additional tools that allow people to understand and harness their natural tendencies, enabling them to achieve interpersonal intelligence and creativity.

Personally, I'm what's termed a high or initiating Quick-Start. In about 90 percent of cases, I have a high tolerance for risk and say yes to tasks before I've thoroughly planned them out. I'm also a low or counteract Fact Finder, meaning that in roughly 30 percent of cases, I'll simplify details and aim for generalizations of data and the big picture ("Essentially, what the study is saying is that eyewitness testimony is unlikely to be accurate"), instead of the analytical precision of a high Fact Finder ("In 57.35 percent of cases, eyewitness testimony failed in the greater Los Angeles metropolitan area").

Without coaching or understanding of natural MOs—Fact Finders and Quick-Starts, for example—might see themselves as natural enemies. That's because high Fact Finders require detail in order to take action and can often lapse into analysis paralysis, unable to move beyond calculations and research. My natural inclination, however—to seize the present opportunity and act—can strike my fact-finding counterparts as reckless and unnerving.

But once aware of our natural tendencies, we can transform from natural enemies to productive collaborators. The truth is that different MOs need one another to achieve results in team settings. Productive teams require a diversity of MOs—someone to focus on scientific proof and detail, someone to distill the essence of research and translate it into action, and someone to follow through and help implement various objectives.

I encourage all my clients to conduct a Kolbe synergy coaching report, by which they can assess whether groups have healthy team synergy or not, so as to avoid *cloning* or *missing modalities*. On a lopsided team, like one with ten members being Fact Finders, is one of high cloning—you can expect analysis paralysis to occur and everyone to feel great about it. Fact-finding clones will kumbaya over nonstop research, geek out over strategy data, and never cross the finish line. If we replace some of the clones with "missing modalities," like a simplifying Quick-Start or initiating Implementor, we can achieve team synergy—and organizational results.

TOWARD BRIDGING THE NATURE/NURTURE GAP

I could write an entire book on the topic of human nature and how it manifests itself in our workplaces. But this discussion provides a baseline. Rooted in these concepts of human nature, the following chapters help bridge the nature/nurture divide by using the 6 Facets of Human Needs at Work and on Teams. We begin with clarity. Clarity of role and purpose can make the difference between success and failure.

SIX
FACETS
of
HUMAN
NEEDS

CONFIDENCE CLARITY CONNECTION CONTRIBUTION CHALLENGE CONSIDERATION

CHAPTER 3

Clarity

"I look at the human life like an experiment. Every new moment, every new experience, tragic or otherwise, is an opportunity to gain a more accurate perspective and helps lead me to clarity."

—STEVE GLEASON

One weekday morning, two to three months into my tenure at an internet start-up, I'd reached my breaking point. It was 2000, the economy was humming, and our investors had finally given us enough money to move into a crisp new building. But sitting in my fancy new office, I stared blankly at my computer screen, realizing I had no idea what to do. I was too ashamed to venture out and say, "I need some direction. What do you want from me?" Such a plea for help, I figured, would be interpreted as weakness.

My struggle for confidence and social acceptance at this organization was surprising because I knew exactly what the organization needed. I was clear on the larger strategy of internet development, how to launch a company at this stage, and how to align this mission with concrete deliverables. But I was unclear about my specific role, so I sat there as time ticked away, feeling progressively more defeated. Finally, I broke down and cried.

A coworker, who had recruited me to the organization, entered my office and asked what was wrong.

"I'm not sure," I replied, "and I don't normally cry at work. But I'm frustrated and can't get a bead on why."

"You know how this entire industry works, Jeanet. So let's flip the script: What do *you* want from this opportunity?"

It was great advice, and I tried to take control of the situation. Ultimately, I couldn't achieve clarity on my own and left the company.

Employee/organizational misalignments like these constantly occur in our organizations. And it's a pity because they leave great employees feeling baffled, frustrated, and even hopeless. Bad fits also cost our organizations untold sums in employee turnaround. According to Deloitte, our organizations fork over $200 billion each year filling vacant positions.[17] Sometimes the employee is at fault. I'll often hear leaders and managers declare, "I'm glad they left. They couldn't do it!"

Oftentimes, however, a lack of clarity is the culprit. In this internet start-up, I was misaligned with my leader, who harbored unspoken expectations that resulted in confusion. If the manager had given me clear directives, instead of a blanket mandate to "lead strategy," I could have thrived. Instead I was left wondering: What type of strategy? Organizational strategy? Where's my beginning and end? What's our timeline and the budget?

During our hunter-gatherer days, lack of clarity on the savanna was dangerous. Imagine our early ancestors enveloped in fog, unable to discern whether the chatter they heard in the brush was birds or a saber-toothed tiger ready to pounce. In a later historical era, lack of clarity is likely to result in the disaster I recounted about the bully and the mentor-now-boss who bought into the bully's tactics. I'd started that role with enthusiasm and understanding, but at the instigation of the bully, people started changing the company's interpersonal dynamics, modifying the business plan, and acting in unhealthy ways—alternating between grand gestures, like fruit baskets, and obscenity-laced teardowns. Amid such lack of clarity, I withdrew.

This chapter outlines important details about organizational and team-based clarity, identifying common missteps. People on teams sorely need clarity, or they'll lapse into confusion like I did. Specifically, team members must understand the purpose of the team itself, their role within it, the team's outcome goals, and how this team fits within the larger organization. If all team members have clarity about these items, detailed below, confusion can't set in. But if there's lack of clarity on some, or even one, of the topics I address below, confusion will reign and wreak havoc.

KNOW YOUR "WHERE"

Many leaders believe that strategy is their exclusive purview and that subordinates' roles are largely to implement strategy. I'm certainly not speaking for all organizations or all leaders, but in the Business Laboratory at Business Alchemist, and throughout my career, I've noticed this assumption to be widespread. A leader often believes that employees won't understand the larger vision or will get derailed by the minutiae of revenue projections, profit goals, and the like.

Even when leaders are committed to communicating strategy, these are often "one and done" initiatives that aren't repeated or reinforced. One email or PowerPoint presentation won't cut it. To achieve clarity, strategy must be communicated multiple times, across multiple media. Strategy statements must be catchy and compelling, shorn of stale leadership jargon that requires an advanced degree to decipher.

In the late 1990s, I remember serving in several strategy meetings. The objective was simple enough: to create an annual plan with forecasted projections for the next five and ten years out. Our meetings lasted around ninety minutes, with each of us endlessly debating the definition of goals, objectives, and strategy.

"What's the difference between strategy and goals?" one person often asked.

"A strategy is totally different than a goal," another responded. "The business books and all the research are clear. I should know: I went to Harvard."

That's right: we had a veritable brain trust of Ivy League–educated leadership strategists, all director-level or above, all recipients of impressive accolades and achievements, and all charged with developing an organizational business plan. And yet, they couldn't agree on basic definitions of objectives, strategy, and goals. Deeply entrenched in their own belief systems, they couldn't arrive at common ground and took several meetings just to arrive at working definitions.

Eventually, we arrived at some workable definitions. It took assembling a row of whiteboards and everyone offering a definition of these concepts in turn. After much heated discussion and the airing of opinions (sometimes couched with elite degree credentials), the team leader eventually selected the final, working definition for how this business planning committee would approach these concepts. We therefore achieved some modest alignment at the team level. Unfortunately, this initial clarity soon vanished because as time passed, and we began the work of business planning, everyone reverted to their original beliefs and expectations. Midway, we caught on and began repetition exercises. Each meeting, we agreed, needed to begin with a baseline repetition of core concepts.

"Remember, we're here to plan strategy. And to review, that means ... " the facilitator would say, rehearsing the definition.

Such clarity, achieved through repetition, is sorely needed in our organizations because it addresses a vital human need. When we shield others from strategy because we figure they won't understand or don't need to know, we deny a need just as vital in our workplaces today as it was to our hunter-gatherer ancestors thousands of years ago. If our ancestors didn't confer around the campfire to strategize about how they'd feed the group, then each individual would be left wondering whether they were tasked with gathering berries or stalking bison. Absent such role clarity, they'd feel blind and fearful of the unknown. A lack of mission clarity often results in fear-based paralysis within our companies too. Employees often see a shift in corporate direction that doesn't make sense to them. But that's because they were never let into the larger scheme, nor their role within it.

I have indelible memories of feeling blind, thanks to the trust builder that my college sorority sisters hosted each year with new recruits. Please understand: I do not endorse sorority or fraternity hazing of any kind. At the time we looked on this as a team-building activity, and it was innocent enough in its outcome. The sorority blindfolded new members (pledges) and told them that they were going to be dropped off somewhere and had to find their way back to campus. "Bring a quarter," we were advised, so that we could use a payphone if necessary. We were blindfolded with no plan, road map, or larger purpose for the exercise. Talk about lack of clarity! As you'd expect, fear kicked in, as did isolation and frustration. All the pledges could do was hope one of the blindfolded girls had a passing acquaintance within the larger surroundings so we could find our way to safety. As it turned out, they drove us around until we ended up at a large monument at night that inspired awe—not dropped off and abandoned. This was an exercise that really bound us to our fellow sorority sisters, and luckily, someone was always watching out to ensure we were never in any danger.

The same logic holds in our organizations: if someone is familiar with the larger organization's strategy and its envisaged implementation, they'll possess the vision and clarity to guide themselves through obstacles or small misunderstandings that inevitably arise. Even if they don't understand every task and step along the way, they can trust in the larger purpose and visualize the final outcome. Some of the sorority pledges had inside knowledge that they'd be blindfolded, and guess what? They knew the larger purpose of the exercise (to foster cohesiveness and trust), and they remained calm and focused as soon as the exercise began. When they removed their blindfolds, a peace and happiness descended on them. Some even described the exercise as profound and moving. When the blindfolds were removed, many discovered that they had never been that far away from home and had actually ended up someplace quite amazing. That's the poignant part of the story and its application to our organizations: even when you feel completely lost, you never are really that far apart. It just feels like it sometimes *because you lack clarity*.

> **Even when you feel completely lost, you never are really that far apart. It just feels like it sometimes *because you lack clarity*.**

In our organizations, for example, we've developed team-building exercises that are completely safe but have just as powerful an impact. I was part of one ten years ago in which we all closed our eyes and stood in a circle together as someone wrapped string and twine around us. We then had to navigate this mess together, finding our way out of the thin, ropy strands in the dark, only relying on one another. Lacking any visuals, this required clear communication—and some of us weren't even allowed to talk.

"If you don't know where you're going," quipped Yogi Berra, "you'll end up someplace else." In other words, you'll wander aimlessly. Corporate strategy plans, however, constitute our "where." When we have clarity on corporate mission and strategy, understanding our "where," we can satisfy the human need of clarity and feel confidence and trust in our organizations.

PHD SIDEBAR

DR. TRICIA'S TAKE

Bridging the gap between nature and nurture by understanding the need for **clarity**

Human beings have a need for clarity. Achieving it can be quite difficult. Ironically, even the definition of *clarity* is rather ... *unclear*. Even the *Merriam-Webster Dictionary* contributes to the issue, defining clarity as "the quality or state of being clear."[18] It's no wonder teams and individuals struggle with the concept. The definitions and research on the topic are anything but clear!

Finding a better definition of clarity. The opposite of clarity is confusion. Psychologists define confusion as a mental state of being disoriented and the inability to think clearly.[19] It's not just internal disorientation that is a concern. Persisting in a state of confusion has a real impact on performance.

When confused, individuals are significantly less capable of effective teamwork. They can't think sharply and struggle with reasoning current circumstances and making the best, most logical decision regarding solutions. Taking the definition of *confusion* into consideration, a better definition of *clarity* would therefore be "achieving the necessary alignment to make effective decisions based on logic." Such alignment strategies include having a "true north" and access to information needed to determine the best action. Once in a state of clarity, one can more effectively reason through any information at hand and arrive at the best, most logical solution.

Clarity is often confused for certainty. Perhaps because we are wired to look for patterns and find predictability as an aid to survival, it is alluring to treat clarity the same way—as a puzzle to solve and an answer to forever possess thereafter. However, the danger in confusing clarity and certainty arises from the ever-changing environment organizations so often experience. As our brains scan our environments with an assumption of predictability, any piece of information that signals inconsistency jumps out. Even a minor inconsistency signals uncertainty, which activates an error response in our orbital frontal cortex, resulting in attention taken away from the goal pursuit and redirected to analyzing the inconsistency.[20] If we seek certainty in work environments, the ever-changing environment will keep our brains in a state of error. Clarity, as a state, instead offers a framework for individuals to function effectively within a state of ambiguity.

Conceptualizing clarity as a state means we must understand it as a condition rather than a destination. In other words, clarity is not achieved once and always a "given" thereafter. Clarity is a condition that can change based on environmental factors. Truly shifting our understanding of clarity in this way means we must focus on the factors preceding a state of clarity. If an individual or team lacks clarity, explore where prior common ground has evaporated. If we treat the state of clarity as a measure of homeostasis in a team, all members of the team become equally responsible for achieving or detracting from the ideal state. Consider a team like an ecosystem where each part of the environment has a profound impact on the outcome. Likewise, a state of clarity depends upon a team actively contributing positively and actively managing negative impacts on the overall state of understanding, taking into account any other environmental (internal and external) factors.

Clarity should not be assumed as a constant and should be treated as a conditional state requiring active management by all team members.

ACHIEVING INDIVIDUAL CLARITY

Once we know the projected "where," each person must understand their part in the journey to get there. Whether we're taking a family vacation to Europe or planning the next phase of space travel, everyone involved must know their role. Absent clearly communicated expectations and requirements, team members can't discharge their roles.

As I've observed countless times, a lack of individual role clarity often results in inaction. I recently observed an innovative leader who created endless confusion on his team. He was a poor communicator, resulting in multiple people with identical requirements and expectations on the team, all working at cross-purposes. The leader withheld the details and purpose of his larger plans, unknowingly pitting people against one another instead of fostering collaboration.

His team was failing him, and at a loss, he asked for my help. In one session, I zeroed in on the problem: baffled and bewildered team members who had no idea about their roles. When I questioned him, his reply was even more perplexing: "Yeah, I'm purposely doing this because I want to see who steps up and becomes leaders. I want them to own it!"

His expectations weren't sinister. This leader had a purpose in mind: he was shielding everyone from information to help them realize latent leadership potential. "I'm going to test them," he figured, "and let them rise to the occasion." Unfortunately, he didn't realize that by denying the human dimension of role clarity, he couldn't unleash this potential.

"This is not going to get the results you are looking for," I told him at our meeting. "They need to have clear expectations and requirements."

I thereafter went about translating this leader's hidden expectations into clear and mutually agreed-upon role requirements. It was a deceptively simple approach. First, I asked the leader to articulate the larger vision for the team—the where—to the group. I then took each team member in turn and, to the leader, said, "What do you expect and require of this person?" I didn't move on until the role was crystal clear and there was mutual buy-in. Some responded with relief, along the lines of "Now I feel so much better. I understand what to do. I kept failing and I didn't know why." Another team member, who was only six months into her role—barely past the first leg of onboarding— and already flailing, had a different response. She was still finding her bearings in the organization, let alone this team. When her turn arose, and the leader conveyed his expectations, she pushed back.

"That's unrealistic," she said, and we arrived at a realistic set of expectations for her.

Absent this two-way negotiation, confused human beings are forced to make assumptions. We do it in our personal lives all the time. How many of you have harbored expectations that your romantic partners would do the dishes before you arrived home or attend your recreational baseball game and enthusiastically cheer you on from the sidelines? What happens when you express disappointment, either directly or passive aggressively, when these people didn't satisfy your requirements? Let me guess: your partners are probably baffled, saying, "What? I didn't know you wanted me to do the dishes or spend my Saturday in the stands." It wasn't clearly communicated and agreed upon before—and the result was hurt feelings and even anger. Sometimes these dysfunctional dynamics can become damaging: "Well, I really thought you would invite us to Thanksgiving, and when you didn't, I figured this family's falling apart."

Wrong! No one reached out for Thanksgiving, and there were incommensurate expectations. Aunt Sally likely figured Mom would do it because she always had, and Uncle Joe made other assumptions because they lacked clarity.

When we make our expectations clear, we not only avoid interpersonal drama, family feuds, and dysfunctional teams, but we also save a lot of money. I was staggered to hear how much when I recently read the results from workplace resource start-up Bravely.[21] Per their study, "70% of employees are avoiding difficult conversations with their boss, colleagues, or direct reports," and, per a 2016 VitalSmarts survey, "every single conversation failure costs an organization $7,500 and more than seven work days."[22] These statistics are flooring. And to make them even worse, they don't take into consideration the human toll of operating in tense, dysfunctional workplaces. We're paying way too high a price for lack of clarity.

In order to address this human need, I once again recommend

one of the clarity tools in my arsenal: Kolbe. I introduced the power of Kolbe in chapter 2, discussing how this modus operandi assessment helps predict how individual human beings will act, react, and counteract in the workplace (and world). It's an especially useful tool when it comes to individual expectations within team settings. For example, I had recently done a Kolbe A Index assessment with the innovative, if misguided, leader I described above who was withholding details and testing his group. After administering the Kolbe test to everyone there, I explained that he was dealing with a mixture of Fact Finders, Follow-Thrus, Quick-Starts, and Implementors, all of whom had much different ways of responding to strategies, plans, and individual expectations. Fact Finders, I conveyed, are especially averse to blind leaps of faith and require access to detailed information; Implementors, by contrast, need to understand the material in a tangible, actionable way; Follow-Thrus are different still, needing to understand the means of getting from point A to point B. High Quick-Starts would be more tolerant to the testing he was doing, while it might lead Fact Finders to tears. Once he became aware of the MO diversity in his team, he could become a much more effective team leader. That's why Kolbe is a clarity tool that I can't recommend highly enough.

To paraphrase business leadership guru Jim Collins, everyone in the organization should know the purpose of the organization and why it deserves to exist. That applies to our teams as well: each member must understand their role on a team, the reason for the team's existence, and its projected goals and outcomes.

CLARITY OF PROCESS

But even when you understand your organizational strategy and your particular role in bringing it about, you can still feel siloed. We might have a series of quarterbacks, receivers, and defensive linemen on the field, all occupying their various positions and knowing the ultimate goal at hand. Nonetheless, the processes and procedures for how to make each play might still be opaque. After all, we know the NFL pays top dollar for the best coaches who can select the best talent and devise the highest-level strategy. But just as with our organizations, the devil's in the implementation. How do we operate in unison, protecting our quarterback if the ball gets dropped, all the while still getting to our collective goal?

Clarity of process is sometimes less grand and more tedious than strategy. Consider clarity of timeline, a major component of process clarity. We might all have a big end date for a product launch or analogous goal. But the microtimelines to get there might be less clear. Vague projections like "sometime this year" won't cut it. We need detailed and specific goals like, "The first part needs to be done by the end of January, the second part no later than the end of Q2."

We probably all remember Wells Fargo's sad tale of corporate mismanagement. Between 2002 and 2016, the company engaged in a practice called "cross-selling," according to which employees, desperate to make unrealistic performance targets, opened fraudulent accounts in customers' names and signed them up for fake credit cards and other payment programs.[23] In the process, these banking employees forged signatures, damaged client credit scores, and made financial transfers of client moneys without their permission. I was reminded of the case because in February 2020, in the middle of writing this book, the *New York Times* announced that the Securities and Exchange Commission had finalized its settlement with the bank—to the tune of $3 billion.[24]

On the one hand, this looks like a clear case of corruption and dysfunction. I must agree with Nick Hanna, US attorney for the Central District of California, who commented as follows: "This case illustrates a complete failure of leadership at multiple levels within the bank. Wells Fargo traded its hard-earned reputation for short-term profits, and harmed untold numbers of customers along the way."[25] I see this as leadership failure at the highest rungs.

But lower down, I read this story as a lack of process clarity as well. As late as 2019, well after the scandal was exposed and the most excessive practices stamped out, employees still described themselves as existing in a pressure cooker. For the company's Des Moines–based workers specializing in debt collecting, the pressure to handle more calls and recoup more money kept mounting—going from thirty calls per hour and $34,000 per month in December 2018 to thirty-three calls and $40,000 early the next year.[26] "For us front-line workers, there's an overwhelming sense of frustration," said Mark Willie, a Des Moines office worker. "There is a general fear of retaliation for speaking out."[27] Other employees echo this sentiment, reporting to the *New York Times* that they feel pressured to disseminate documents that they know contain falsehoods, all to meet deadlines. When it comes to corporate ethics, performance targets, and sales perks, employees cite a widespread culture of "doublespeak."[28]

In many ways, the Wells Fargo tragedy speaks to all of the themes raised in this chapter. It speaks to a larger failure of corporate strategy, both in terms of ethics and in terms of mission. Without this larger strategy (the "where"), employees were blinded by a series of ever-increasing performance goals (unable to agree or buy in to individual requirements), scrambling to meet them in unrealistic time frames and increasingly unethical ways (lacking clarity of process). I'm sure that many frontline workers knew something was amiss with cross-selling, just like current employees in Des Moines reported in 2019. But they existed within a larger dysfunctional system that was entirely opaque, murky, and confusing. As human beings they had other needs—like supporting families and paying mortgages—and probably went along with these dubious strategies to satisfy these goals. They operated in the fog of uncertainty and lack of clarity. Tragic losses of corporate reputation, purpose, money, and individual well-being were the results.

Sometimes the fog of confusion can compromise your organization, demoralize your people, and cost you precious resources.

Sometimes the fog of confusion can compromise your organization, demoralize your people, and cost you precious resources, like it did for Wells Fargo. But sometimes it just wastes valuable time. One of the organizations that employed my services, for example, formed a committee for marketing. "We're going to throw six of you in a room, and we want you to figure this whole marketing thing out."

Six months elapsed, and the committee was still struggling, making no headway on marketing. After coming on board as a consultant, I asked "What's the purpose of this committee? What outcome are you trying to achieve?" It probably comes as no surprise that the committee lacked clarity on these questions. When they sat down and tried to arrive at an objective, I observed an utter lack of alignment on these questions. Some team members thought the objective was to create a website, while others believed it was to attract new clients, while others still believed they were focused on attracting referrals from existing clients. They all had different ideas about what the outcomes should be, all stemming from the bewilderingly different definitions of "marketing" they all had.

I gathered everyone around a whiteboard, and we agreed on the semantics of marketing and from there developed a common language, addressing different initiatives and projects and how they might start to come together. This involved repetition: before every meeting, the leader would announce, "So this meeting's objective number one out of our five is X, and what we're trying to do with it is Y, and the people involved are A and B." And then they asked themselves questions to achieve clarity of where and when.

And they saved time and money. This group had met one hour a week for six months and achieved nothing. If you do the math using average values of $100 per hour, then this cost the organization $600 per week for twenty-six weeks—nearly $16,000 in total! But once they achieved clarity and began producing, their efficiency (not to mention morale) skyrocketed.

Carol Minges, the CEO of First Financial Credit Union, understands the importance of clarity more than anyone I know.

When she assumed the role of interim CEO in 2013, she inherited an organization deeply in need of clarification. The company had a mission. But that mission was untethered to a purpose, meaning that the credit union's employees couldn't understand and really own it. The company also lacked strategic and business plans as well as core value and vision statements. This lack of clarity was exacting a detrimental toll on the company: the organization was suffering financially, the culture was poor, and employee morale was weak. It probably comes as no surprise that this new position caused Carol some considerable stress and anxiety.

In the summer of 2013, Carol convened the credit union board and executive team for its first planning session, writing attributes and key ideas for others arrayed around a white-board to reflect on. At the time, the stated mission directed toward members of the credit union, was "Save you money; make you money; save you time. That's why we exist." While the mission was solid, employees needed to know the "why" of the mission—in other words, they needed a purpose. The new purpose was far more inspirational: to help people achieve their financial dreams. That mission and purpose gave way to a vision: to grow by providing the best member and employee experience in the communities the credit union served.

What a big step. Instead of employees entering the workplace every day with the mission to make their members money and maybe save some time, they now understood the underlying purpose. "But we were still," reflects Carol, "looking through a very fuzzy-looking glass with respect to our vision." That's understandable: it's great to have a compelling mission and vision statement. But it must become living in the orga-nization. And the vision was so vague that everyone couldn't align behind it and get energized. In the days to come, the credit union experienced inconsistent success.

As a newly minted CEO, Carol first had to address bol-stering the company's financial performance. Some execu-tives thought they should pursue a technology direction, while others were committed to a service path. These different ideas were exacerbated by a lack of managerial focus: everyone was passionate about their individual pet projects. These projects were well-meaning, and many were valuable, Carol conceded. "But absent clarity," Carol said, "there's no way to harness and direct that passion toward a common, positive goal—something vital to achieving strong financial performance, engagement, member experience, and community impact."

In 2019, the credit union hired me as a coach, and I guided the executive team through a challenging exercise: devise a targeted one-page outline of the company's vision and put a business operating system in place. There's something clarifying about condensing this information onto a single page. Suddenly, the company's vision wasn't vague and up for interpretation, as the page crystallized and clarified everything.

One target was attaining one hundred thousand members. By comparison, the institution had only thirty-four thousand at the time. The company had a very risk-adverse, data-driven CFO who first balked at the thought of it. "Impossible," he said. But it gnawed away at him, and eventually, gazing at that piece of paper, it excited him. The CFO had harnessed his passion in the service of the organization, and it's been exciting for Carol to see him fueled with passion for this major milestone.

The other leaders followed suit, and instead of focusing on twenty to thirty diverse projects, they followed my advice and forecasted their three to five priorities for the following quarter. Everybody in the organization focuses on this cluster of priorities each quarter, which are now meticulously quantified and tracked. And because everyone inevitably gets off track from time to time, the company organizes weekly meetings, helping project, management, and executive teams regain focus, if necessary, and keeping everyone in alignment with achieving quarterly goals.

Under Carol's leadership, the company traded its milquetoast core values (knowledgeable, accountable, responsible, ethical, and service oriented) for something more energizing. The new core values of each member were serving as brave, bighearted banking nerds who do the right thing, with hustle. Carol remembers how that vision initially gave everyone goosebumps. And it deeply resonated. Throughout the organization, people now reminded one another to be brave, urging them to have brave conversations with coworkers instead of avoiding them. "Oh yeah," someone will often say, after a gentle nudge from a coworker, "I need to be brave and talk to John, don't I?"

Clarity, it turns out, requires accessibility. When employees want to learn something new, they read a book together, celebrating their core value of being banking nerds. And when the COVID-19 tragedy struck the company, the workforce celebrated being bighearted by devising ways for employees and members to access emergency loans and capital to keep their households and businesses afloat. Carol's story illustrates that when a workforce galvanizes around something accessible, engaging, and compelling, magic results.

Under Carol's leadership, this organization has infused clarity into its very DNA. As a result, business and morale have both skyrocketed. In their 2019 TINYpulse surveys, which measure employee engagement, the credit union came out on top of industry benchmarks for every single month of 2019. The credit union also achieved record financial performance, community impact, and net promoter scores in 2019. Absent clarity, Carol concedes, none of this would have been possible.

If you are leader at a midsize company wrestling with any of the clarity issues I discuss in this chapter, use this exercise tool liberally.

CLARITY TOOL

In order to provide clarity in your communications, emails, presentations, etc., I recommend this framework:

1. **Context.** Set up what you're going to say! Why are you sharing this information or direction? What is the purpose of the communication?

2. **Content.** Share it directly. What is the project or information being shared in simple, direct terms? What is the strategy,

vision, and plan? Does every team member have clear and agreed-upon expectations and/or requirements? Have you clearly outlined the where, what, when, how, and why?

3. **Conclude.** Repeat what you said, and add clarity to the action. Does everyone know their role in the project, mission, or process? Are all expectations and goals clearly stated with definitive timelines and deadlines?

CONFIDENCE CLARITY CONNECTION CONTRIBUTION CHALLENGE CONSIDERATION

SIX
FACETS
of
HUMAN
NEEDS

CHAPTER 4

Connection

"The business of business is relationships; the business of life is human connection."

—ROBIN SHARMA

or the last few years, I've worked closely with a doctor's office, trying to run a healthy medical practice, where all stakeholders are connected. My medical clients especially struggle with this. While medical doctors are top rate, arriving at their practices equipped with medical degrees and PhDs, they often haven't received business training. Medical solopreneurs or small partnerships tend to struggle as they transition to more complex partnerships, entailing new challenges of business development, finances, and people management. My client is no different. It has multiple locations throughout the rural Midwest, recently added a slew of new doctors to the payroll, and has grappled with handling this growth and dealing with tension in its larger culture.

When I first observed the practice, I immediately noticed how isolated everyone was. The technicians, doctors, and office staff kept to themselves, functioning more like independent contractors than members of a team. To create the synergy necessary to run a successful business, I'd clearly have to dig deeper and distinguish the root cause of dysfunction. After further observation, I found that while each location was jointly responsible for the firm's financial success and market reputation, one location of about ten staff of nurses, doctors, and administrators identified as the underdog. And it had slipped into dysfunction. Negative talk and complaints permeated the office, as doctors felt they spent undue time "listening and fixing" to interpersonal problems, detracting from the time they could spend with patients. Accountability, responsibility, and productivity all waned as these doctors faced burnout.

If they could just fix this underdog location, this practice believed, everything would improve. It wasn't that simple, I told them, as the real problem was a broad disconnection across all locations. As well-trained physicians, I explained, they were trying to fix the immediate bleed but were neglecting the internal source of the problem. The practice hired a company that guided everyone through team and culture-building exercises intended to bolster the culture and help people understand how to work better, build connections, and communicate.

These nurture-based activities, predictably, provided some short-term relief. People began communicating better with one another and even rallying around some core company values. As we've seen in past chapters, these nurture activities are great. But if they come out of sequence, preceding nature- or need-based interventions, they are premature, providing a short-term adrenaline rush before organizations slip into old patterns. These activities served as a valuable kick start to get everyone energized to embark on a larger overhaul. Once people were momentarily taken out of organizational dysfunction and complacency, we could address the larger problem of belonging—a human nature need—at the root of the problem.

My work with this medical practice serves as a powerful lens to analyze and address the core human need of connection. Though physician practices struggle with a unique set of challenges in the business landscape, they typify many of the challenges of running a partnership-based business outside of core business spheres like accounting and law. They also represent the proverbial canary in the coal mine. While widespread worker dissatisfaction and burnout plague our workplaces in general, these forms of dysfunction afflict physicians in particular, compromising the mental health of providers as well as society's collective health. But without focusing on what binds or connects people together, dysfunction seeps into our

Human connection is indispensable to healthy teams and is premised on connection to common core values, physical place, and a larger company culture.

organizations. Regardless of your industry or market niche, human connection is indispensable to healthy teams and is premised on connection to common core values, physical place, and a larger company culture.

DR. TRICIA'S TAKE

Bridging the gap between nature and nurture by
understanding the need for **connection**

Human beings are wired for connection. For decades, psychologists have explored the link between individuals and the others around them. At the beginning of the twentieth century, Russian psychologist Lev Vygotsky stated that "we become ourselves through others" and dedicated his career to studying the cultural and interpersonal experiences of development.[29] Over one hundred years later, neuroscientists at the NeuroLeadership Institute have helped elucidate the biology of connectedness.[30] Their studies examining human behavior using neuroscience techniques (e.g., using functional magnetic resonance imaging to measure brain activity by detecting changes in blood flow to areas of the brain) support how people define themselves in relation to their "in group" and "out group," providing further insight into "othering."

Othering. "Othering" is the process (sometimes nonconscious) whereby an individual identifies another person as either part of their "in group" (some call this their tribe) or the "out group." Biophysiological evidence of the importance of "othering" provides compelling reasons to pay close attention to connection on teams. Different areas of the brain are activated when you think about someone within your group versus someone you perceive as an "other,"[31] and your ability to empathize with someone drops significantly when you consider them as a competitor or outsider.[32] Research also shows that from the other person's point of view, simply feeling left out (or "othered") produces brain activity that mirrors physical pain.[33] Essentially, there is more truth to the saying "It hurts to be left out." There is also evidence of the importance of connectedness at a brain chemical level. This research also shows that an increase in oxytocin level correlates with an increase in collaborative behaviors. Increases in what may even be considered minor collaborative behaviors matter; activities like watercooler talk have been shown to increase productivity in organizations.[34]

Humans are herd animals. We seek safety in numbers. People tend to take their social cues from the majority as a way to maintain their own well-being, which can be great in the example of safety in numbers; it can also have negative consequences, like when mass market shifts lead to stocks crashing.[35] If individuals feel safer surrounded by their group, what happens when team members find that they have lost favor with the team? According to research around human needs in work group settings, people have an instinctual reaction to try to get closer to things that feel rewarding and farther away from things that feel threatening. When team members find themselves "othered," their fears of disconnection are activated. Humans, as herd animals, have a tendency to rally around the decision to "other" someone who has failed the group in some way.[36]

How can we meet the need of connection in the workplace? NeuroLeadership Institute suggests buddies or mentors. This can help outsiders integrate into groups. Providing one safe relationship and a source of comfort to ease the threat response increases the likelihood of the offending individual changing their behavior and feeling that there is a reason to do so.

CONNECT TO CORE VALUES

You can think of core values as your organization's guiding principles. No matter what top talent you recruit, no one will feel connected if you don't share these frameworks and principles.

Many organizations approach core values in a superficial way. To use a construction metaphor, many companies neglect their building's foundation, structural beams, and engineering supports, skipping straight to the fun stuff like picking out window treatments and glossy new kitchen appliances. They paper the organization with well-articulated and high-strung core values statements, print out glossy photos with them, and emblazon them on corporate websites. That's not a problem—they've simply skipped a crucial step. We must first construct our entire business edifices around core values, laying the foundation and bearing beams, before we get to landscaping and crown moldings.

We must first construct our entire business edifices around core values, laying the foundation and bearing beams, before we get to landscaping and crown moldings.

Best-selling author and leadership guru Patrick Lencioni first alerted me to the importance of core values in his now classic *The Four Obsessions of an Extraordinary Executive* (2002). Among other qualities, he instructed, top executives are obsessed with core values, integrating them into hiring decisions, performance reviews, and other basic company procedures. They appear not only on marketing literature and posters but also feature in group meetings and are the subject of praise ("That's a great example of X core value, Tommy. Well done!").

Perhaps the Mayo Clinic represents the best and most moving example of living core values with authenticity and effectiveness. If you're looking for a benchmark in organizational core values, I must highly recommend *The Mayo Clinic: Faith—Hope—Science*, PBS's two-hour documentary on the Mayo Clinic, with Ken Burns as producer and director. The Mayo Clinic exists on behalf of and filters all decisions through its core values. It aligns teams around them and only hires doctors and staff who wholeheartedly embrace them. The proof? Mayo hires the best in the world and pays them a below-market salary. You come to Mayo for the mission and not the money.

While many hospitals prize a "patients-first" ethos, Mayo's patient-centricity trumps financial concerns and logistics. Consider this: the clinic broke from many industry leaders and brought the diagnostic laboratory and the surgical theater together. Why? Cancer patients who undergo the surgical removal of tumors must wait agonizing weeks or months while their samples are transported to the laboratory for testing. In conformity with their core values—though perhaps not their P&L statements—Mayo invested in uniting the machinery and laboratory because that was in the best interests of patient care. Patients-first always pays off for Mayo, and when you go there, you know that you're getting rock star doctors serving you. For over a century, the Mayo Clinic has leveraged its core values to achieve extraordinary outcomes, putting this institution on the forefront of innovation and clinical care.

When core values are well executed, they address the human need of belonging. Whether you're a patient enduring a terrible disease, a world-class oncologist, a surgical nurse, or one of the Mayo Clinic's countless community stakeholders, you feel a sense of belonging when in the Mayo ecosystem. That sense of belonging and belief translates into better medical outcomes. If I walk into any hospital in the world right now that's not Mayo and read a sign that says, "We put patients first," I question it. Whether fairly or not, I can't really believe it unless it's Mayo.

My small client practice in the Midwest was no Mayo Clinic, but they were doing their best when it came to core values. When they encountered toxicity on the team, they were able to return to them and use them as a springboard to address other challenges they were experiencing and to which we now turn.

CONNECTION TO PLACE

For a doctor's office operating in the rural Midwest, connection to place is a glaring problem. Here's the problem my client medical practice faced: after investing so much money in recruitment and employee training, how could they retain their top talent?

You couldn't blame employee flight. Bracketing the larger dysfunction, there was nothing binding these physicians to the larger location. Most physicians in the practice performed their duties with patients, attended some perfunctory meetings, and then returned home. None of them struck up spontaneous friendships with their peers or suggested informal social outings. Office staff similarly spent little time with their peers outside of the patient room. They never engaged in casual conversation, let alone had coffee, lunch, or spoke about their families to one another.

During a brainstorm session, I also discovered that they weren't connected to the larger community. As new doctors recently transplanted to the area from their medical school or residency programs, these doctors lacked any preexisting geographical ties to the area, making this place a perfect breeding ground for sadness, loneliness, and other terrible afflictions, like depression, that disproportionately afflict physicians. The practice had basically said, "Come here from the city, land in rural America, and get no support from your new work community."

My first round of solutions was predictable enough. These doctors needed to spend more time together personally. The practice began with community involvement and outreach. If one of the doctors expressed an interest in recreational activities or hobbies, the staff arranged a bowling night or weekend hike. If they had spiritual inclinations, they introduced them to new church communities. Senior physicians began extending dinner invitations to their younger counterparts, breaking bread with them and their families in informal settings. Once this social activity got rolling, they involved community stakeholders like Realtors, who took the young physicians around the area showing them prospective properties. They began learning about the history of the place, its major attractions, and its local institutions, making them feel an enhanced sense of rootedness and belonging. The new physicians now had a connection to the place and the people that created a bond to the organization.

Countless academic studies, covered in the news media, highlight the role of technology and connection. They lament how the rise of cellular phones and social media technologies have increased our digital connections throughout the world but have unfortunately decreased our interpersonal connections, actually reinforcing our collective loneliness and isolation. The statistics are frightening. Between 2009 and 2017, suicidal ideation among high schoolers increased a whopping 25 percent, as actual suicide, anxiety, and depression rates rose steadily as well.[37] Ditch your cell phones and social media accounts, these studies seem to suggest, and you can welcome more connection.[38] I am in accord with these findings, and subscribe to non-digitally mediated forms of connection, particularly when cementing team dynamics. But there's an important caveat: it's not simply the absence of technology but the presence of geographical place that's decisive for connection. And it's always been that way.

Global cultures have long emphasized the importance of sacred or special geographies, interweaving them among their belief systems. Geographical landmarks exercise a particularly strong hold among indigenous populations in America, as do churches and civic institutions today, providing concrete places to connect and build relationships. In 2015, two Princeton economists stunned the country when they released their study on "deaths of despair" among white males without college degrees, who were living shorter lives. While these deaths of despair were marked by increased use of alcohol, opioid drug abuse, and suicide, the authors understood these as symptomatic of a larger problem: a lack of connection to important social institutions like marriage, the labor market, and so on.[39]

Throughout my career, I've led many virtual teams. Before modern videoconferencing software like Skype and Zoom, which enhance human connection, I led conference calls with success. I've found that if properly maintained, this communication can be very powerful, enabling geographically diverse people to collaborate. But I also found that if we convened in person, even if only once a quarter or twice a year, this enhanced our bonds considerably. That's because we can concretely appreciate the humanity of our fellow collaborators.

Let me share an example. In 2019, I flew to Dallas to connect with sixteen of my colleagues who work in the Entrepreneurial Operating System® (EOS®), the system I teach in my coaching work. We're all independent solopreneurs, dispersed throughout the country and usually without reason to collaborate. Over the course of a weekend—beginning on Friday, when we didn't know one another, and leaving Sunday—I felt like I'd made some of my best friends in the world. Over lunch, dinner, dancing, and special events like glass-blowing classes, we came together, realized that we all had common struggles and now understand how to collaborate with and support one another.

One day we engaged in a "whisper walk" exercise, in which we were all blindfolded and circulated throughout the group, whispering in one another's ears the one thing we each needed to hear most ("You're smart and capable," "You're great at what you do and people value you," and so on). It could be something that was preventing us from moving forward in our business or personal lives ("head trash," as we like to refer to it, or "self-defeating narratives," as it's sometimes referred to in the self-improvement literature). Whispering in someone's ear is such an intimate experience, only heightened by lacking sight and talking about difficult topics. In this exercise, we metaphorically saw one another's vulnerability. It was a profoundly moving experience—and when I boarded the plane back home after that weekend, I was so grateful that instead of having a virtual team, I enjoyed human connection and professional intimacy with people who understood me and wrestled with similar struggles.

While I strongly connected to my EOS colleagues, my physician client and their recruitment initiatives are preliminary, and time will tell if they retain these young doctors. But if the research is any indication, this practice will soon enjoy increased retention, particularly when doctors feel connected from day one. According to a *2018 Retention Report: Truth and Trends in Turnover*, over one-quarter of Americans left their jobs that year. And that's a pity, because this turnover could have been prevented. Per the study authors, "More than three in four employees (77 percent) who quit could have been retained by employers."[40] While they cite many reasons that such attrition could have been prevented, connection to place plays a central role. When companies focus on retention during the early onboarding phase, making new recruits feel connected to the organization, their colleagues, and the physical location in which they are embedded, problems with retention fade. But as the study also suggested, a connection to company culture is just as important to place.

CONNECTING TO CULTURE

Connecting physicians to a larger culture, however, is a particularly acute problem. Traditionally, the medical field almost creates forced disconnection and dysfunction. Many believe, nobly, that they need to simply focus on their patients and that cultivating a larger culture among physicians would somehow compromise patient care. "It's all about saving lives," the mantra seems to go; "everything else is secondary." Like our corporations in general, moreover, the medical establishment has traditionally been very hierarchical. Everyone ascends the ranks from intern to resident, to attending on their own, deferring to higher-ups, and separating themselves from the other ranks. Just like the younger generation in corporate America is experimenting with flattened managerial styles and power sharing, so, too, the younger generation of physicians is struggling against this culture of isolation.

This all means that when I began work at this practice, I encountered a group of physicians highly connected to a larger mission and purpose—practicing medicine to save lives—but disconnected from one another. One of the first things I did with them was guide them through my 6 Cs. When we arrived at connection as a need, a whole host of issues rose to the surface, mostly involving culture. Because of the unilateral emphasis on patients and personal career growth, a lot of dysfunctional behaviors, like codependences and mental health problems, had festered. Perhaps most tragically, in losing connection with one another, the physicians were experiencing burnout. Burnout is a huge problem, which, according to a CareerBuilder survey reported in a 2019 *Forbes* report, afflicts a stunning 61 percent of workers.[41] In my physician practice, such burnout resulted in doctors' disconnection from their patients. The doctors recounted stories that are all too common today—patients saying that their doctors didn't want to connect with them and build a relationship but simply viewed them as a constellation of symptoms to treat and diagnose. We realized we needed counseling before we could build the necessary connections to sustain a healthy work culture.

They were primed to hear this news. A valuable physician, integral to the entire practice, had just left. The practice proved unable to reconnect her back to the team, and in recounting this story to me, there were tears, punctuated by moments of levity and laughter.

"You know, we really are good people at heart," one of the physicians shared with me, reflecting on losing this person. "We've just lost our way."

"This is beyond my pay grade as a business coach," I said to the team. "This goes deep."

We recruited a group counselor/coach to achieve a positive goal. Their goal: To become a functional medical practice.

It's a noble goal, and from personal experience I know how difficult it is. In the introduction, I described a brief period when, ten years into my consulting business, I was ready for a new challenge and embarked on a new opportunity in good faith. What I didn't mention was this experience was with Bill, my mentor of two decades, who assembled this team. "I'm getting my band together," he said at the time, a smile on his face. He'd assembled his favorite collection of workers—his professional dream team—and believed we'd all magically mesh.

The analogy Bill used is telling. You've probably heard many stories about the infighting that plagues bands and how conflicting visions can spell disaster and breakup. That's exactly what happened here. Bill recruited the best guitarist, the best vocalist, the most experienced drummer—and everyone wanted to be Mick Jagger. With too many Jaggers, all with strong visions for what the songs should look like, how the tempo should go, what the performance venues had to be, we ended in disaster.

"I got the best people together, and you all get along with me," said Bill, baffled. "I thought you'd all get along."

We did all get along—*with Bill*. But we were never forced to build a culture among ourselves. Everything flowed through him, and we fell into a dysfunctional dynamic of trying to constantly please Dad—we were working at cross-purposes. It became part sibling rivalry, part *Lord of the Flies*—a dysfunctional dynamic of unhealthy codependencies with the guru in charge, instead of broad-based collaboration.

GETTING TO KNOW YOU

To prevent your workplace from going the way of dysfunctional medical practices or rock bands on the skids, you need to connect. There are many trust-builder and team-builder exercises on the market, with my colleague Patrick Lencioni and others providing invaluable tools. But I've found particular success with my own human-needs-centric, getting-to-know-you exercise. I call it the 3-2-1.

It's simple: as a team leader, have everyone in a group share three events they've experienced, how they responded to them, and how they impacted them (preferably non-wedding-day or birth-of-child related). Next, ask them to share two stories from childhood or coming-of-age adolescent memories. These two stories will give you a glimpse of their cores. Many react to these pivotal moments with fear and learn from the experiences. So my last directive is this: share one of your biggest fears. Some of your people might initially softball these answers, sharing that they are afraid of performing on stage or harbor an irrational arachnophobia and wince every time a spider ambles by. But many people go deeper.

When you share such experiences and your reactions to them, you can delve into people's core—a springboard for talking about human nature. Nature and needs tend to surface in these questions. This is a great way to begin talking about the 6 Facets of Human Needs (6 Cs) and getting people to relate to them in a personal way. You can of course conduct this exercise over WebEx or Zoom, but it's most resonant and powerful in person.

While the 3-2-1 is a great way to begin constructing your vibrant and healthy human team, follow it up with a one-on-one alignment exercise. During this activity, after everyone is already primed for professional intimacy, we share our challenges and strengths together and work on solving whatever needs fixing to achieve connection. These are real eureka moments, interpersonally speaking. This is the equivalent of having the "difficult conversation" and often proves so illuminating.

"We never knew why we didn't get along because we actually have a lot in common," people will say exiting the room.

After achieving alignment, relationships can take on enhanced clarity, and petty squabbles evaporate. As Phil Stutz and Barry Michels write in their *New York Times* best-selling *The Tools*, if we're willing to endure a period of brief pain, a normal human experience, we can achieve enormous psychological breakthroughs and prevent pain over long periods of time.

Our personal lives bear out this truth all the time. How often have you heard of two family members who've been estranged for their entire lives who finally reconnect and become vulnerable with each other at the end of their lives, faced with a death in the family or a major sickness? They end up seeing the conflict for what it was—a lot of assumptions and miscommunications that tragically curtailed a great relationship. During these alignment exercises, I often hear two things:

1. "We really don't know why we were so at odds for so long."

2. "I wish we'd talked sooner, because we could have fixed this."

Tara Kinney, CEO of marketing and revenue operations company Atomic Revenue, might be known for her expertise in growing and scaling companies. But I like to think of her as an expert connector. And I'm not the only one—she's been a connector for most of her career, and she's frequently interviewed about maintaining business connections, especially in virtual environments.

These talents were hard earned. Tara spent six years working as a recruiter, interviewing dozens of people a week, and honing her internal radar for selecting talent for diverse organizational and team settings. She had to match each business owner or team leader with an individual candidate's background, skill set, and potential to perform on different project teams and in diverse business settings. That, in turn, involved balancing such factors as emotional intelligence, personality, and expertise. "If it's a tech-savvy client, you can't have someone on the team who doesn't understand technology," reflects Tara, "and if a team leader is more old-school analogue, you can't assign a digital native or Generation Z influencer as their main point of contact."

Later, as an independent consultant, Tara mobilized these skills to help smaller companies scale. After investors had granted them capital, founders hired Tara to advise them on how to use it. It was a daunting task, as Tara created the processes, data, technology, and the labor plans for fulfilling their growth commitments to their investors. Once again, she needed to recruit people to help with every aspect of the business including revenue operations, marketing, and sales. Tara inadvertently became one of the early directors of the gig economy as she found the right freelancers with the right skill sets to perform jobs required within her labor-planning schedule. In working with companies all over North America, she found that personality and work style were substantially more important when assembling teams than technical knowledge and work experience. Someone might be technically proficient or expert in doing a job, but if they couldn't connect with others it didn't matter.

Those skill sets provided the foundation of Atomic Revenue, where she leads a team that aligns people, processes, and data for profitable organizational growth. Atomic Revenue tends to work with smaller owner-operated businesses, requiring diverse team members to augment the capabilities of center anchors, who oftentimes are power leaders. "That makes connection even more important," says Tara, "because if team members can't connect with one another as humans, or if they're unable to effectively collaborate on opportunities, the entire team dynamic can fall apart." And Tara's extensive expertise also confirms that less is more. "If it's a working group to accomplish a tactical project or strategic direction, we recommend eight people or fewer," says Tara. "More than that, and you start to lose some of the productivity and decision-making effectiveness."

Tara and a partner cofounded Atomic Revenue in 2015, and synergy existed between the partners for several years. As is true with many owner-run small companies, the role of founders evolves as a company scales over time. The experience became more personal for both Tara and her founding partner when they encountered evolution within their own company.

As initial camaraderie between the partners began to diminish, connections with team members across the organization began to fray, and Atomic Revenue hired me to coach them through this challenge. We began by drafting a structured process for running their business. Unfortunately, these efforts magnified the company's lack of connection across the organization. Both partners recognized a now permanent and irreversible problem. After negotiations, a mutually acceptable solution was reached allowing Tara's partner a suitable exit path to depart the company as both an owner and employee. In the process, opportunities were created for other team members to become official organizational leaders.

After the negotiated resolution was finalized in January 2020, connection, energy, and productivity exploded at Atomic Revenue. The company's pipeline of sales opportunities tripled within two weeks. Digital "watercooler" talk spiked. Atomic Revenue doesn't have a centralized office where employees and contractors congregate—its forty-person organization is dispersed throughout the country. The company therefore has digital communities and technology services designed to connect everyone outside of their specific project groups. During the latter stages of 2019, these channels had dried up a bit, but once the underlying partnership headwinds were resolved, the company's Slack activity increased as people began to organically and spontaneously initiate relationships with their colleagues. "It was as if the inability to connect with leadership inhibited everyone else's confidence to connect with one another," Tara reasoned.

Everything seemed to change. What's so amazing to me is that nothing about the company dynamic has changed other than the unification within the leadership team. All communication and engagement with teams and individuals have remained the same. But new team members and consultants simply materialized, asking to join, while others spontaneously connected with one another. Tara's still trying to figure out the secret sauce but understands that connection hinges on organizational leadership. "Every individual person feels such a deeper connection to the company and teams that they feel free to connect with each other in ways they were previously uncertain about," said Tara. "I feel like a huge weight has been lifted," Tara says. "I don't feel the burden of carrying all of the responsibility and accountability and instead can rely on a tightly connected team shouldering it with me."

Every month, the company hosts a popular digital happy hour over the videoconference medium Zoom. There's only one rule: no two people from the same location can log in together. Everyone must attend as individuals to decompress, get to know their coworkers, and highlight specific team-member accomplishments or company milestones of the past month. Tara admits that digital happy hours were a tough sell to some of the executive-experienced team members but immediate hits with the digital natives. The senior strategist team had more "productivity-focused" agendas while the subject matter experts embraced the "relationship-focused" intent of the digital happy hour concept.

The company has platforms to learn about the professional skills and capacities of others, Tara observed, but digital happy hour and similarly styled events represent opportunities to connect, build rapport, and develop trust as a foundation for successful project teams. When people collaborate on projects, happy hours ensured they wouldn't begin work as strangers but instead as colleagues, familiar by face, voice, personal style, and unique background. When the COVID-19 tragedy shook the workplace, everyone went to Slack to share stories about challenges they encountered during quarantine, like balancing work with childcare and

Wi-Fi router enhancements. They also shared silly memes and commiserated about staying home all day with spouses, kids, and pets. This further cemented trust and camaraderie. And as Tara has observed, most skepticism has now faded, and everyone sees the value of making these personal connections with their virtual colleagues.

She's actively planning for the future, inviting a diverse group of people to join the leadership and ownership team. Thanks to these efforts, she now enjoys a management team comprising three generations, with tech-savvy millennials on one end, seasoned baby boomers on the other, and Generation Xers like Tara in the center, connecting the value of experience on both ends of the spectrum. Rooted in human connection, this company has vast potential.

Are you doing regular team and/or trust builders with your teams? If not, please do so. And consider these questions as well:

1. Are you sharing the plan, strategy, or vision on a regular basis (either once per month or once per quarter)?

2. If the team member or employee is not from the local area, have you given them information about the local community? Or have you involved them in the community?

3. Do you have a strong meeting cadence as a team? Are you committed to regular and consistent meetings?

4. Do you eliminate technology from your meetings?

5. Is the group/team size fifteen or under to maintain intimacy and vulnerability?

SIX FACETS *of* HUMAN NEEDS

CONFIDENCE
CLARITY
CONSIDERATION
CONNECTION
CHALLENGE
CONTRIBUTION

CHAPTER 5

Contribution

"Every person has a longing to be significant; to make a contribution; to be part of something noble and purposeful."

—JOHN C. MAXWELL

Size matters. Especially when it comes to teams. That's what Mona Sabet discovered in 2012 when she opened nonprofit networking company Hipower.[42] That year the company led ten female executives through intensive workshopping, coaching, and storytelling services, and years after this experience, they all still felt enduring trust and connection with one another. But when the company grew and these mentoring-coaching groups began to swell, Sabet noticed a decline in group cohesiveness and effectiveness. It's then she learned an important lesson about team intimacy: human purpose, empathy, and performance all hinge on group size.[43]

Scientific discoveries confirm Sabet's findings. Anthropologist

Robin Dunbar, for example, correlated the size of an animal's brain to the number of social connections it could maintain and effectively nurture. The famous Dunbar number is 150 for all social connections. Does this resonate with you? Do a little experiment and begin looking around at different groups of people. These could be groups of anything, from the number of people your company employs in one of its overseas factories to your own Christmas or holiday card list. You might find that these groups top out, at least in terms of closeness and intimacy, at 150.[44] According to Dunbar's research, furthermore, human beings can visually identify about 1,500 people, have about 500 acquaintances, enjoy 50 solid friendships, and maintain 15 close, intimate connections.[45] And that magical number of 15 applies to groups and teams as well. "Beyond 15," observes Sabet, "empathy starts to evaporate and a sense of common purpose decreases. Factions may start to develop."[46]

As managers and directors, we intuitively understand Dunbar and Sabet's findings, but we still let our teams swell. Instead of sticking to manageable teams of three to seven, or even ten people, we pile others on, oftentimes for personal and political considerations. We need to reach a certain diversity and gender thresholds, we think, and we must include Bob from accounting. *He'd be hurt if we didn't.* I don't want to dismiss these factors—diversity, for example, undermines "groupthink" and spurs innovation. But when we include too many people, we ultimately damage the team, the company, and the individuals involved. And that's because the larger the group is, the less each individual can meaningfully contribute.

When it comes to achieving team intimacy and performance, size comes first, and the correct people to fit such teams a close second. When we select the right people for the right-sized teams, magic can result. That's because when we're arranged in small groups of optimally functioning people, we can fulfill our human need to contribute. Small-team intimacy triggers the love hormone, or "cuddle chemical," called oxytocin, which bonds us to people and promotes human connection.[47] With this sense of connection in place, we can contribute to a larger goal and mission. Contributing to a larger purpose is among the greatest of human aspirations, approaching the pinnacle of Maslow's hierarchy of needs: self-actualization.

Research continues to corroborate the principle of "smaller is better." A 2013 Gallup study found that smaller businesses had more engaged employees than larger ones.[48] If a company had ten people or less—the approximate size of an optimal team—42 percent reported feeing fulfilled (while only 30 percent of their larger corporate counterparts reported the same). The "Ringelmann effect," named after a twentieth-century professor of agriculture, helps explain this logic. Professor Ringelmann asked people to perform a deceptively simple task: tug on a rope. He discovered that the more people he asked to pull, the less effort they expended. Later theorists derived the concept of "social loafing," "relational loss," and the "bystander effect" to describe this phenomenon. That's just academic language illustrating a fundamental and intuitive human truth: the more people pulling, the less one feels their own contribution and the less other people know they're contributing. Ever wonder why people don't help out in major automobile accidents, refrain from voting, slack off on big teams, or don't contribute to the rope-pulling contest at the annual county fair? It's the Ringelmann effect!

The logic of the cohesive small group also underlies Amazon founder Jeff Bezos's two-pizza rule. If you can't feed a team with two pizzas, he says, it's too big.[49] More than two pies, and everyone won't feel equipped and empowered to make individual contributions— and, metaphorically speaking, they'll stop tugging on the rope. When it comes to creating teams of contributing individuals, I'm a strong proponent of inclusion (i.e., having groups of different people who all feel and experience a sense of inclusion). Your team might achieve great diversity, but how comfortable is everyone to contribute? How much will these members want to expend 100 percent of their effort to pull on the rope? I strive to create small, highly productive and inclusive teams so that, when in positive climates, each member can contribute to their fullest.

Following Dunbar, Sabet, Bezos, and my five-hundred-plus observations in the Business Laboratory, I suggest that teams never exceed fifteen people. When it comes to leadership teams, departmental teams, or boards of directors, the optimal number is probably three to seven. The higher the team ascends in the organizational hierarchy, the tougher the decisions become, and fewer people involved means confidential information is protected and fewer people need buy-in. Fifteen, however, should always be the tipping point—over that number we can't achieve critical vulnerability and meaningful collaboration. Over that number, we can't satisfy our human need to contribute.

DR. TRICIA'S TAKE

Bridging the gap between nature and nurture by understanding the need for **contribution**

Human beings have a need to contribute. We crave the ability to create impact and forge meaning. It's not enough, however, that we benefit ourselves alone; we also seek to do work that matters to other people. Researchers have found that individuals who report feeling fulfilled by their jobs are far more likely to feel their work is tied to a greater good.[50] Since, on average, we spend the vast majority of our time at work, it makes sense that human beings seek greater impact through contribution to their work teams.

Amygdala hijack and work. If we want to contribute, why do we sometimes mess it up and indulge in conflict instead? Even with the best intentions to make a positive impact, we are still driven by a strong internal force to protect our sense of self, and this is where the amygdala comes in. The amygdala's function is necessary and often positive. However, your amygdala does not care about the right setting, the right tone, or choosing the right words in a work situation.

In fact, when your amygdala becomes triggered, your brain is overrun by a nonconscious process that works faster than your rational brain. It spurs you to make an impulsive, instinctual decision before you can think it through logistically. Acting on instinct is great when a large animal is about to attack; it's not so great when your teammate has just hit your last nerve by missing an important deadline. When events like this arise, your brain needs energy to assess the threat and determine action, and your amygdala accesses this energy by diverting blood flow from your prefrontal cortex, the region in your brain responsible for logic and reasoning.[51] This region of your brain helps you be a professional adult. But under its spell, your brain disregards all of your training, education, and coaching retreating to a more primitive and reptilian state.[52] This part of your brain is not interested in care, consideration, reasoning, or planning and only interested in base needs like physical survival. Unfortunately, with your amygdala hijacked, you act poorly.

Do not act with only your reptile brain. Actions taken with your reptile brain are usually not the smooth and conscientious. Luckily, your brain does not desire to stay in such a survival-only state. Evolution has given us a quick recovery from this hijack, and your brain begins to recover in only about six seconds.[53] Prior to that, when blood flows away from your prefrontal cortex, your capacity to make good choices decreases. This is roughly analogous to decreasing ten to fifteen IQ points, or becoming 10 to 15 percent "dumber" in that moment.[54]

What can you do to not fall victim to your very speedy and sometimes overactive amygdala? Do not act when you are hijacked. Take a moment before you respond with your words, tone, or actions. I will often tell coaches that they need some space between their initial internal reactions and their outward choices. I advise people to use questions as a tool to get to that space. Choose a good open-ended question to gain more information in the moment, and allow yourself to breathe and count to ten.

Clearing the way for positive contribution first means not falling victim to amygdala hijack.

THE EVOLUTION OF A TEAM

In 2016, I began coaching an executive ownership team at a privately held, high-innovation organization. Eighty employees strong, all of these technical experts had STEM specialties at the master's or doctoral level. They'd formed the company about five years prior, and I coached them for about two and a half years.

The team began with the two founders and gradually accumulated several more—the company progressively acquired more owners, and company ownership emerged as the sole criterion for team participation. This group of owners struggled to make important business decisions because they lacked role clarity and didn't know how they should contribute. As an operationally focused team, they could all confidently speak about creating or delivering a product or service but knew nothing about running or promoting the business from the back office. They also lacked voices from marketing and finance. Instead of such discussions, each topic became a five-person debate at best, or knock-down-drag-out fight at worst. This team earned a dubious honor: the most exhausting client I've ever coached.

My initial eighteen months with the team were excruciating. I was only with them about four to five session days a year. But even that was nearly debilitating. There were no low-stakes or simple conversations, as every basic decision we encountered devolved into conflict and distraction. They cut one another down and undermined one another's points, eagerly pursuing distracting tangents instead of staying on task. The entire team suffered from attention deficit disorder. We agreed on a functional structure for the team together, assigning different people to different roles, each of whom made distinct contributions. We also assigned one team leader to facilitate meetings, set the agenda, and exercise a veto function on important decisions. Predictably, everyone liked the idea of team leadership in theory but in practice refused to report to the team leader we'd collectively appointed.

Refusing to vest leadership in one person, the team lacked accountability. I observed a very primal situation unfold. These leaders' prefrontal cortexes knew that power sharing was the right course, but their amygdalae strenuously disagreed and expressed strong fear when their control was taken away. The toxicity mounted. Three of the members bickered incessantly, one of them froze, and one of them fled.

"I give up," one said, leaving the room.

The rest watched him go and kept fighting. This lasted a year.

I did some more wrangling, and one of the cofounders became the team's core leader. Though it made them uncomfortable, they eventually relinquished control. I seized the positive momentum to suggest we draft a team charter, outlining how the team would handle conflict, promote the best in everyone, and so on. Team charters are modest documents, usually consisting of around ten to twenty bullet points. Over the course of two hours, we debated the parameters of our charter.

"Work for the greater good," suggested one member. Then the rest debated.

"Does each one of you work for the greater good?" I questioned everyone. "By that I mean, do you make decisions based on the company, and not for your own department, ego, or financial benefit?"

As it turned out, they didn't work for the greater good. I was impressed by the team's candor. Often, when a coach or facilitator poses a question like that, most people will say yes, whether they're lying or not. While they weren't entirely committed to their organizational vision, they all decided they wanted to form a cohesive leadership team, take responsibility for the organization, and use the charter to help them run an effective business.

First on our charter was a commitment to use the tools and system that I facilitate, teach, and coach—the Entrepreneurial Operating System. That was needed, they decided, for the team to perform at its best. Secondly, they were to assume best intentions on the part of their team members. And that meant they had to fundamentally change the way they interacted. Instead of bombarding one another with accusations and immediate dissent, everyone discussed how they'd like to receive feedback. The freezers in the group, I discovered, were Kolbe high Fact Finders—and you can't browbeat people like that into submission. They need facts and figures—and many of them on this team requested this information be delivered in a nonhostile fashion. With enough detail, these people could join their Kolbe Quick-Starts to solve problems. Others registered a certain sensitivity to difficult topics. For that reason, the group charter stipulated that before people were delivered tough news, they'd alert the group.

We debated the terms and semantics of this thirteen-point charter. The language was important, and after we agreed on it, everyone complied. The group circulated copies of the charter for everyone, tacked them up in the conference room, and tucked some away with their materials each meeting. If someone violated the charter, it was readily accessible for consultation.

I introduced some facilitation toys to help translate these principles into practice in a playful, if corny, fashion. I circulated a stuffed elephant throughout the room. Whenever someone had a proverbial "elephant in the room," they announced it, clutching the plush toy as they delivered the news. We also rotated "sacred cows," and if someone began politicking, they'd promptly receive a "dead horse" thrown in their direction. The dead horse was a sign meant to convey, "The poor animal is dead. Stop beating it!" The charter was the breakthrough this team needed to set some guiding principles and commit to them. And the toys didn't hurt.

Having traded toxicity for this guiding charter, the team could then focus on the hard work of performance ahead. Remember, this is a team of individuals not working for the common good. That proved clarifying for performance because once they started communicating, the group understood the organization's mission: to sell to a large corporation as soon as possible. They all united under this joint mission and thenceforth contributed to it. Over the next six months, their joint contribution was considerable. They performed steadily and diligently, working around the clock until a large corporation purchased them for a higher multiple value than the company had been worth two years prior.

It was gratifying to see how healthy and happy they were. When they entered meetings, they smiled at one another. Don't get me wrong: they didn't like one another and weren't invested in the longevity of their joint enterprise. But that makes it even more remarkable: they were all able to contribute, and all got what they needed, which was an external acquisition. And instead of purchasing a dysfunctional mess, the new organization inherited a functional company with a solid leadership team at the helm. Absent this team's ability to contribute, the company would never have sold for such a high value, let alone left a legacy of a functional, high-performing organization.

Though this team's evolution from toxicity to high performance might seem unique, or at least particular to its own industry and special circumstances, it actually followed a typical developmental pattern of all teams. In 1965, psychologist Bruce Tuckman postulated five stages of team development: forming, storming, norming, performing, and adjourning:

TEAM DEVELOPMENT STAGES

- Little
  agreement
- Unclear purpose
- Guidance and
  direction

FORMING

- Agreement and
  consensus
- Clear roles and
  responsibilities
- Facilitation

NORMING

- Task completion
- Good feeling
  about
  achievements
- Recognition

ADJOURNING

STORMING

- Conflict
- Increased clarity
  of purpose
- Power struggles
- Coaching

PERFORMING

- Clear vision
  and purpose
- Focus on goal
  achievement
- Delegation

As we observed, the initial "forming" stage of this team saw little agreement, purpose, and direction. The only threshold for participation was ownership, and absent nonfinancial buy-in to the mission, everyone was at sea. This led to a lengthy "storming" stage—though perhaps unusually difficult for this group, it isn't called storming for nothing. For a year, conflict and power struggle hung like storm clouds above the oval conference table. In fact, this team almost stormed me right out of the process. Sometimes the conflict was so intense I wondered what purpose I was serving. But I also knew that the dysfunctional fighting, fleeing, and freezing occurred because everyone couldn't contribute in a healthy matter.

At the storming phase, teams can progress if they seek out increased clarity through strategies like external coaching. And after struggling through the lengthy storming season, we finally arrived at "norming." At this point, we formed the team charter and ran Kolbe assessments on everyone. Because this was an elite team of owners, we couldn't address the Kolbe clones in the room and reconstitute a diverse group of Kolbe MO types. Our teams don't always enjoy this degree of flexibility, especially ones in leadership. But we operationalized the power of Kolbe simply by understanding it. Having awareness of each person's MO inclinations allowed us to form a charter responsive to everyone's needs (some needed facts and figures, others needed to deliver larger visions, and so forth). That was the breakthrough moment as the charter enabled everyone to cohesively unite and contribute to the team and, by extension, the larger organization.

Norming is a pivotal period in any team's evolution, as it serves as the midway fulcrum leading from disunity to performance and adjournment. That's exactly what happened in my group. Kolbe became a tool to navigate the strong egos in the room, while the team charter served like a mini core principles statement, guiding the tenor and spirit of the teamwork to follow. In 2012, Google ran Project Aristotle and found something similar. In analyzing over one hundred teams underway at the tech conglomerate, they found what intuition might suspect us to

Only in such a climate of "psychological safety" can individuals feel free to collaborate and contribute.

believe: "The best teams are mindful that all members should contribute to the conversation equally, and respect one another's emotions. It has less to do with who is in a team, and more with how the members interact with one another." Only in such a climate of "psychological safety" can individuals feel free to collaborate and contribute.[55] That's exactly what happened for my team. Having already realized they weren't interested in the organization, the team devoted six months of intense "performing" around a different mission: selling the enterprise. They all felt good once it sold ("adjourning") and they could dissolve the team and pursue other causes—perhaps causes to which they were committed.

Based on my work in the Business Laboratory, and the pivotal nature of norming in the evolution of teams, I've come to recommend the use of team charters to most of my clients. This team developed one late, after years of trauma and conflict. Don't wait that long on your team. Every team benefits from a rough charter that simply addresses baseline questions about why this group of people has come together, its ultimate purpose, and how everyone might work together to create success. When teams proactively create charters, they become functional from the start.

When we don't exercise such proactive prudence at the initial team "forming" stages, everyone loses out. I once coached a real estate company that appointed a star employee to join a leadership team. She was among the founding generation of employees and beloved throughout this company. The team director believed she'd be hurt if not included. But no one was clear on what she needed to do, and while everyone else gelled nicely, she began to quietly suffer. She didn't have the requisite skill level to intervene on topics of substance, and every time something went awry, she felt blamed for it.

"I just don't know what to do. I don't know what you want from me," she said one day, dejected.

Eventually, after everyone asked her what they could do to help, the employee said she felt that the best way for her to contribute was to leave the leadership team. She admitted that she was personally arresting the progress of the team, and to compound the problem, her lack of contribution was making her feel bad. This was a challenge she couldn't handle, and she'd only agreed to it because of her connection and commitment to the organization. After this realignment, the leadership team was the right size and comprised the right people, armed with clarity of purpose and the ability to contribute. This employee now contributes elsewhere, according to her skill set, and both she and the company are better for it.

We're all guilty of making emotional decisions like this. My background in marketing has taught me what neuroscientists have documented with precision: human beings make largely irrational decisions based on emotion, instead of rational evidence. Gerald Zaltman, a professor of business administration at Harvard, concluded that emotion accounts for a stunning 95 percent of consumer purchasing![56] Janet Crawford, one of the globe's leading experts on using neuroscience to improve our businesses, confirms that 90 percent of all behavior is subconscious in origin.[57] "We are more slaves to our biology than we realize," she says. But with knowledge comes power. As team leaders, we should encourage our members to seek out those primal hints. You know what I mean: that lurking, uneasy feeling that a polished presentation made great business sense but was somehow off, or that sense of terror and fright we get when forced to encounter new ideas.[58] Luckily, Crawford subscribes to the major premise of this book: if we can understand our underlying biological impulses—our human needs—we can leverage that knowledge to create more synergistic teams (not to mention happy team members).

In my story about my mentor, Bill, I shared that absent clarity of role and social connection, I was no longer able to contribute. I couldn't believe it: me, the industrious member of the team, brimming with enthusiasm and orchestrating major decisions at the ground level of the organization, had quickly spiraled into complacency. That hinged on my lack of contribution. When I didn't feel like my natural abilities and skills were being leveraged to positively contribute to my team, I gave up.

When human beings are robbed of their opportunity to contribute, they'll often respond in one two ways: they'll withdraw, like I did, or they'll engage in frenetic action, chasing shiny objects that distract everyone. In other words, they'll check out, or they'll contribute in ways that are utterly distracting or even counterproductive.

By addressing our human need to contribute, for example, we can achieve higher ROIs. No, I'm not just talking about the return on your investment capital in that latest patent or innovative product. I'm talking about the "return on individuals." Dave Bookbinder, author of *The New ROI: Return on Individuals* (2017), devoted his career to measuring the value of intangible assets, especially human capital. He and a colleague were convinced that if properly managed and developed, employees could become happier and more productive, ultimately driving company performance.[59] I agree, and I believe that ROI hinges on people's ability to contribute. Contribution allows each person to move from withdrawal, or passive contribution, and to level up to the team—a rising tide lifting all boats. That means that everyone expends their maximal effort instead of doing the bare minimum (i.e., pretending to pull on the rope but instead slacking off and thinking about their Twitter feed as they pretend to grunt). This creates positive multiplier effects, endowing people with new capabilities that ultimately result in enhanced team and organizational performance.

One of the best things we can do as leaders is acknowledge the human psyche's need to contribute and reward it. Follow the lead of my high innovation ownership team and ask about every team member's preferences when it comes to communication and encouragement. We'll discuss this topic more when thinking about the human need of consideration (chapter 7). But for now, if you take this simple step, you'll place yourself above the rest. According to a 2016 Gallup report, one-third of workers have received recognition in the past week, while "at any given company, it's not uncommon for employees to feel that their best efforts are routinely ignored."[60] In today's climate of high workplace turnover and a global war for talent, we simply can't afford such low return on individuals.

But just like our world in general, our teams have become less homogenous, more diverse, and geographically dispersed. Just ask Alec, who managed an engineering team at ITT that was located in Texas and New Jersey.[61] These two groups were skeptical of each other. Alec tried in vain to unite them, but when they met a client together, they opted to stay in different hotels, and when he sponsored a joint dinner during this meeting, the two teams clustered together on opposite ends of the table. Knowing he had to improve the situation, he focused everyone around a common goal of creating software to oversee hardware remotely. "He emphasized," notes the *Harvard Business Review*, "that both subteams *contributed* necessary skills and pointed out that they depended on each other for success."[62] With common purpose and a jointly felt sense of individual contribution, the barriers gradually came down, team members began appreciating one another, and they gelled into a functional team. By addressing contribution, Alec's team was able to connect, achieve clarity of purpose, and work together harmoniously. If you assume the mantle of leadership and leverage your role as a leader and team facilitator to address contribution, your teams can do the same.

FROM TOXICITY TO TEARS

My career is now dedicated to coaching others in strategic vision, execution, accountability, and team health, showing how they can achieve high trust, high results, healthy communication, and connection to their organizations. As I've described throughout this book, much of my day-to-day work involves taking leadership teams of small and medium-sized companies off-site four times a year and coaching them through the tough stuff.

Recently, in a generic St. Louis hotel conference room, I had a special experience with four executives. They were all crying! Keep in mind, this wasn't a touchy-feely profession either. It was a no-nonsense bastion of male leadership. It was during the group's annual planning day, and we were focused on team health (as a precursor to organizational health).

In the context of doing some trust-building exercises, I asked the team to share the following as a trust builder: "What life event, personal or professional, has impacted you *most?*"

As academic and best-selling author Brené Brown would say, these male executives leaned into their vulnerability and shared some poignant stories of loss, regret, and trauma. Some, for example, shared that they were once nonfunctional alcoholics or heroin addicts and how others stepped in to rescue them. Another shared that he had lost a child in an accident. Many shared how important their ex-spouses were to them. That was the person who changed them, who allowed them to trust, and they were grateful for the experience, despite the regret they felt for their marriages' ultimate failure. Some shared shame about going to a state college instead of a major university. Sure, they conceded, they might lead a $50 million organization now, but they still wondered why the shame of attending a state school still gnawed at them.

After this collective catharsis, born of collective contribution, we were able to turn to the major challenges the company was facing: What areas do we need to stabilize? What areas do we need to scale? With renewed clarity and focus, we could move from short-term goals to focusing on long-term visions, strategizing about how to stay competitive in a climate of constant market disruption. Our group dynamic embodied the 6 Facets of Human Needs (6 Cs): everyone contributed, felt connected to a vision and a healthy series of challenges, had clarity of purpose, showed consideration to others, and so on. The leadership trusted one another, enabling them to contribute to one another on this team and guide the organization's larger contribution in the marketplace.

Most importantly, this team—and others like it—emerged from this meeting more concerned about the people in their organizations than generating profits alone. They were invested in their most important ROI: return on individuals. As leaders, managers, and coaches, we know that focusing on people isn't always easy. But our best market strategies and plans mean little without people to execute them. Let's focus on them, and allow their contributions to shine, so we can best position ourselves for success.

Shea Peffly has contributed a lot to the business world throughout her career.

In 2008, she began work as director of operations at a small veterans' care company that employed twelve people. The company served veterans and their surviving spouses, helping them access pension benefits from the Department of Veterans' Affairs, pay expenses, secure home care funding, and the like. Shea found the mission extremely rewarding. In addition to the intrinsic meaning and poignancy that comes with helping veterans, Shea's father had served in the military, making veterans' advocacy especially close to her heart.

In 2011, when the company's workforce reduced to five and it rebranded itself to Veterans Care Coordination, Shea was tasked with regrowing and scaling the company. And scale it she did. Over her tenure, in which she served as vice president and then CEO, the company's revenues grew by a factor of twenty-five, and its workforce swelled to over eighty. While the company was in this growth mode, Shea felt a maximal sense of contribution. She worked closely with the veterans personally, and each individual life she impacted simultaneously served to fulfill this organization's mission and inspired other employees to do the same. Most employees had some affiliation with the military, meaning they shared a passion for the organization that only grew the more they collaborated with others to help veterans. As Shea recalls, "Seeing the passion ignite in new employees while seeing them carry the torch forward was simply inspiring."

Everything ran well. "There was nothing in the organization that Shea wouldn't do for another employee," she recalls. And she wasn't alone. If someone was sick or needed special support because of extenuating circumstances, others offered to fill in, with as much passion and enthusiasm as the full-time employee they were temporarily replacing. When everyone assembled for roundtable discussions and was trying to solve a problem, Shea would approach certain team members and express her appreciation for their insight and knowledge. "You're more experienced in this issue than we are. Help us understand this so we can solve the problem," she'd say. It wasn't just lip service. Guided by the nobility of the mission, there was a culture of trust and mutual contribution that guided all activity.

But when organizations scale so quickly, it's hard to keep this spirit alive. Starting around 2015, the company entered a three-year period of stagnation. Shea's leadership team began to crumble, the employees began distrusting their leaders, and for the first time, Shea and her coleader didn't align on business operations. During this time, the company hired me as a coach. Shea longed to understand why they were stuck and had countless conversations with me, asking for guidance on how she could contribute to the changing business and inspire others to contribute effectively as well.

The more she solicited feedback, the more she learned

that her direct reports didn't trust her. The more she probed, the more she realized she was part of the reason why the company was stuck. She wasn't letting go and providing the autonomy her team needed to contribute. She wasn't delegating and trusting in the people she had trained.

Shea metabolized the feedback and made a conscious choice to change her approach. When someone approached her about a project or initiative and asked for the go-ahead, she said, "I trust your judgment. Let me know if you need my support." She stopped checking up on everything and everyone and led through deadlines and mentoring. "Shea, what's the worst thing that could happen?" I used to ask her. This question hit a nerve. Gradually, her one-on-one meetings with employees became conversations rather than the militant-style questioning they had previously been.

Armed with the confidence of their boss to contribute, the new leaders on her team yielded some strong outcomes. And for the first time in thirty years, Shea recalls, she was vulnerable and let go emotionally and spiritually. With strength of purpose, Shea empowered and elevated her team, unleashing their power to contribute. Surprised by this life-changing experience, she then realized that she had taken the organization as far as she could—her next contribution in business would be elsewhere. She therefore stepped aside and looked for her next opportunity to contribute to the world.

Six questions and considerations to meet the need of contribution:

1.   Is everyone on your team serving at their highest and best?

2.   When setting expectations, are you achieving mutual agreement?

3.   Does each team member have a voice at the table? Do you have the right voices at the table?

4.   Is each individual continually learning and then applying new knowledge to the team or organization?

5.   Does the team member feel they are contributing meaningful work? Do they like their job and/or role?

6.   Have you established guidelines for working as a team?

CHAPTER 6

Challenge

"A coach is someone who tells you what you don't want to hear, who has you see what you don't want to see, so you can be who you have always known you could be."

—TOM LANDRY

"Meaning is the New Money," declared the *Harvard Business Review* in 2011.[63] We already knew that. And if we didn't, we could do a quick Google search to find that research has steadily accumulated since that article's publication to substantiate the importance of meaning and engagement in our businesses.

As leaders and managers who increasingly supervise the purpose-driven millennial and Generation Z workforce, we know that the straightforward exchange of money for manpower no longer works. Workers don't just want a paycheck. They yearn for meaning, purpose, and challenging self-growth in their roles. They want it so much, in fact, that employees are now even willing to pay for more meaning: over 90 percent of employees, for example, would exchange a portion of their lifetime financial earnings just for more meaning on the job.[64]

We should all be celebrating this fact as meaningful jobs benefit organizations as much as employees: they save our companies countless sums in annual turnover fees, worker absenteeism, productivity lapses, all the while infusing employees with purpose, mission, loyalty, and innovative potential.[65] In today's markets, characterized by hyper-competitiveness, disruption, supply chain challenges, and constantly changing customer demographics and preferences, we can't afford to have 85 percent of our worldwide workers disengaged.[66] So why aren't our workplaces redesigning themselves to maximize meaning?

I suspect it's because meaning hinges on challenge, something that represents a different type of human need than the ones we've explored thus far. Unlike connection and clarity, for example, we don't always proactively seek challenging, meaningful work—not unless we're on the extreme side of the growth mindset spectrum, always pushing to expand our horizons and always seeking critical feedback. Human beings naturally crave stability, and challenge is tough and risky. Challenge is a human need best described in metaphors: it's the pressure that transforms the grain of sand into a pearl, the larvae into a butterfly, or carbon into a diamond. Meaning is the reward we receive for all of our challenge. Absent challenging pressure, people can't realize their latent potentials. When we challenge our teammates as leaders and managers, we often give them something that they don't even know they need: the pressure to ascend Maslow's hierarchy of needs and reach new personal transformation and professional performance heights.

Unfortunately, leaders and managers often hesitate on challenging others, not wanting to push people or make them uncomfortable.

But when we withhold opportunities for productive challenge, we ultimately deny others an important human need, a human need we almost always recognize only in retrospect. I say that because once pressure has been applied, and our employees witness the outcome—the diamond or pearl—they're grateful and fulfilled. I hear about the meaning and purpose they experience all the time in the Business Lab: "Thank you for challenging me!" "That's just what I needed!" Leaders courageous enough to apply pressure and make people temporarily uncomfortable help them meet human needs they didn't even know they had.

Leaders courageous enough to apply pressure and make people temporarily uncomfortable help them meet human needs they didn't even know they had.

I should know. I've been an Entrepreneurial Operating System (EOS) implementer since 2013. About two years into my journey with the program, I was struggling with certain parts of the business. While I excelled on the facilitation, teaching, and coaching functions of my role, I grappled with the more entrepreneurial business-development side. Once I cinched a client, I was fantastic—but I had trouble promoting myself and my services enough to accumulate them. Though I'd been in sales and marketing for so long, I found selling myself to be fundamentally different, and navigating that was unfamiliar and hard.

Each quarter, my fellow EOS implementers convene in Quarterly Collaborative Exchanges™ (QCEs), where we commiserate, share best practices, and network. During these meetings, we sit arrayed in tables of eight to ten people and, among other things, share our client numbers. This isn't for the faint of heart, as everyone present, knowing your client count and the number of session days you have conducted (what I refer to as "lab time" in this book), can extrapolate your annual income. Though this represents an unusual amount of transparency for the business world, all disclosure is voluntary and done in the spirit of openness and camaraderie.

During one 2015 meeting, I shared my numbers at the QCE, and they were solidly average. I didn't despair. I enjoyed a great life. I was comfortable. Complacent. Jonathan B. Smith (JBS), a highly successful EOS implementer at my table, approached me after this roundtable talk. "Hey, Wade, you're a rock star. So what the hell is going on?"

I knew JBS was a New Yorker, but his bold and direct style still caught me off guard. I'm in an area of the country you might call "Midwest nice," which refers to a demeanor or personality type, typical of middle America, that expresses kindness regardless of the context, meanders around the edges of difficult conversations, and avoids confrontation. Unlike people inhabiting the coasts, Midwesterners don't tend to directly challenge others. JBS, by contrast, bluntly told me that I could do better and wasn't reaching my potential.

With his burning desire to help others achieve their potential and his mantra that "results matter," JBS declared, "You are now my project. I'm going to call you every week and kick your butt."

During our initial telephone meeting, we completed a document together, indicating my growth areas, where I saw future business opportunities, and how I understood my strengths. He also told me that during our weekly calls, he was going to teach me some of the tips and tricks ("best practices") on how to steadily grow my business.

It was initially hard for me to process his intervention. I was briefly nervous about what prompted it and where it was coming from. But after the initial shock, I was soon overcome with a feeling of honor because this successful colleague clearly saw potential in me and was going out of his way to help me shine. I also felt scared, not wanting to fall short of his expectations. That nervousness persisted, especially throughout our first few coaching calls.

I awaited our "Friday kick-ass calls" at the end of each week, when he'd ask me what I'd accomplished that week and how I'd demonstrably improved my "Biz Dev." We'd debrief over the presentations and client sessions I'd conducted that week, poring over what I'd said and whether it was effective. He challenged me to shed some of my Midwest nice and become more direct. After each presentation to a potential client, for example, I'd conclude my remarks and largely leave the ball in their court.

"Let me know what you'd like to do," I'd say to my audience.

This didn't cut it for JBS, who suggested I say, "Does this sound like something you seriously want?"

I heard his larger message loud and clear and knew I needed to transform my passive conclusions to client presentations into something more proactive and inspiring. I had to challenge my potential clients and pry, asking them to take this journey with me to grow their businesses. Being so direct and self-promoting wasn't part of my personal style, but if I wanted more buy-in and greater reach, I had to do it.

JBS's consistently applied discipline, mingled with tough love, and his inspiration and support were exactly what I needed. But that didn't make the mentorship calls and coaching advice any less challenging. I was afraid of my clients perceiving me as brash or pushy, and I was worried that I would waste JBS's precious time if I didn't improve (which was all in my head). Each week I persisted, responding to his challenges by challenging myself. What was my weekly breakthrough going to be? I asked myself each week, applying pressure to achieve something great. During our calls, I gradually asked him for more nuance in his advice and how I could be even more effective.

Each week, my business progressively improved, and within six months of his intervention, which I now know was an investment, it exploded. I'd easily tripled my client count and was officially beyond my capacity. Thanks to his mentorship, I've now entered the EOS Freedom Forum. For this group of top EOS implementers, we get an extra day with EOS founder Gino Wickman, learning about freedom of wealth and freedom of time and other best practices.

Though I've had many coaches over the years, JBS represents the very best of leadership, management, and facilitation. He selected me for a challenge, freely invested his energy and wisdom in me, and helped me achieve new accountability and engagement heights. Of course, it was appropriately tailored to my needs at a certain point in my career. While his tough love was what I needed to transform my business and ascend to the highest rank of EOS implementers, other people might need a softer touch. The point is meeting the need for challenge in a way that can access individual potential.

MOTIONING TOWARD MODERNITY

Sometimes leaders proactively seek mentees individually like JBS, and sometimes market pressures serve as functional equivalents, jolting us out of stale fixed-mindset patterns with scary challenges. That was the case for one of my industrial services clients, who worked in a dying industry. This company's technology had been extremely important in the late nineteenth century. But changes in building styles and architecture had gradually disrupted its traditional consumer base, rendering its expertise less relevant. Older commercial buildings still required its services, but they, too, gradually fell into disrepair or were even demolished each year, sometimes because the costs of maintaining them became too great.

Faced with its rapid financial decline and diminishing industry relevance, this company remained complacent, clinging to what its industry association said in weekly social media blasts and other literature, which largely confirmed a traditional twentieth-century belief system. Unlike other clients who'd pivoted in the face of market pressure, this company seemed committed to its own death spiral. This is a textbook definition of a "fixed mindset." Growth-mindset-oriented companies respond immediately or quickly to challenges ahead. Those on the more fixed-mindset end of the spectrum can take six months—or even six quarters, six years, or six decades to change. That's because human beings and organizations (run by humans) often respond to desperation with self-protection. From a human-needs standpoint, a fixed mindset is a familiar, and therefore psychologically safe, way to proceed. But all wasn't lost with this client.

The company hired me as a coach in 2016, and I interpreted this as a sign that they were ready, however haltingly and timidly, to change course. This was the firm's first acknowledgment that it wasn't responding adequately to the challenges it faced. A culture of complacency had taken hold throughout the decision-making process at all levels. This company, which had mechanical specialties, slavishly responded to its commercial clients, not only performing essential technical tasks but mowing lawns and other odd jobs. These miscellaneous tasks allowed for just enough money to trickle in to serve as a distraction from the major challenges ahead.

Following my initial discovery sessions, the company leadership realized the sobering news: if it wanted to cling to its vastly diminishing market niche, it would have to raise its prices. Absent this, it couldn't remain solvent, even in the short term. If the company wanted to achieve long-term solvency, however, it would have to take a much bigger risk and pivot its existing skill sets to respond to a broader and more contemporary market need. The executive team faced some terrifying prospects: all the company's competitors had gone out of business, its specialty clients could hardly afford to pay more, and investing its limited resources into a new mechanical specialty was risky. This was also a multigenerational legacy company. Did the owners, soon to reach retirement age, want to bequeath an antiquated business, and losing business model, to the next generation?

I'd already decided that I wasn't going to exert pressure on this company. Just like children, adults often resent being told to eat their leafy greens. They might know they'll benefit from the nutrition, but they still find it unpalatable, especially at first. If I pushed the team too hard, like a personal trainer giving his clients too much weight to deadlift, they might pull a muscle and limp away, injured. In addition, if I came on too strong, I risked being the recipient of blame and shame, as distressed people and organizations often respond when they experience fear. I had to plant various seeds of change for how the executive team could stabilize and scale the company but ultimately let the leaders decide.

I didn't hear from the company for a while after we'd revealed these root issues. It took three years before I received a call. In the meantime, the firm's already limited industry relevance had deteriorated further, and it faced extinction. Finally, the leadership made a change and responded by following my coaching, raising their rates with existing customers, and pivoting to a new business model to attract a fresh crop of clients.

BEING TOO NICE

One of my clients similarly delayed its response to a challenge, this time involving personnel. Quarter after quarter, a handful of its employees posed problems. "John Doe," they'd say during our off-site executive meetings, "is our biggest challenge." "Same with Jane Doe!" They all lamented these people and how unpleasant they were. When I probed deeper, I discovered that these problem people were double trouble: bad culture and technical fits, unable to discharge important tasks and fit in with coworkers. But the organization prided itself on loyalty, and the company had employed some of them for decades. Too much loyalty can be a liability, I told them, and these people had become unproductive—even counterproductive to their teams and the organization in general.

"You are a for-profit business, right?" I asked, being deliberately provocative.

"Of course," they responded.

"Then why do you keep people who aren't productive on the payroll?"

They grasped my logic but responded by saying they were loyal to a fault and proud of their reputation for friendliness and kindness. They also blamed me, suggesting that I was tough on people and couldn't possibly understand the company ethos they espoused. When they responded like this, I didn't take the bait and redirected

> **Businesses must always prioritize their most important assets—their people—and show them grace and consideration. But we can't let people problems linger and fester any more than we can let other business issues do so.**

the conversation to issue at hand. It's my job, I explained, to challenge them, identifying the barriers facing their business.

Businesses must always prioritize their most important assets—their people—and show them grace and consideration. But we can't let people problems linger and fester any more than we can let other business issues do so. While my industrial client had become complacent about its product offerings, this one was complacent about its talent-management challenges. Both could end in catastrophe if left unaddressed.

Six quarterlies into my meetings with the executive team, I exercised leadership. I announced to the group that this was the last time I ever wanted to hear the names of these problem employees discussed. If everyone was willing to accept these individuals, so be it, but no more complaining. I didn't even want them identified on the whiteboard any longer. These people were enough of a financial and time liability, wasting thousands of dollars and man-hours already, I explained. I wouldn't allow them to squander any more resources. I then held my eraser above three names on the board. "Accept it, change it, or remove it," I said.

To my surprise, the group decided to remove one. This represented its first firing in a long time. The following quarter I learned that this had been a great decision—everyone was much happier, including the employee. He'd become frustrated because he hadn't been able to complete his work and had become complacent and unengaged. But the money was good, so he figured he'd stick around until retirement. The team discovered that letting him go hadn't been as painful as they'd imagined. They'd even empowered this former employee to lean into new and different challenges in his professional journey.

After courageously overcoming that challenge, the executive team took further action the following quarterly meeting, electing to "change" one problem employee. We arranged a tough coaching discussion in which we communicated that the current professional role was untenable. We challenged him with a different position at the company and enacted measurables that he'd have to accomplish.

If he didn't perform, we said, he'd unfortunately be asked to leave. I don't know the destiny of this particular employee, but I do know the company is much better off. They'd dramatically changed. After six quarterlies (a year and a half) of lost productivity, income, and energy, this company addressed its personnel challenge and had made accountability an integral part of its talent-management function.

Luckily, challenge doesn't have to involve painful moments of reckoning. As managers, facilitators, and project leaders, we can let it infuse the way we give and process feedback with our direct reports. For our teams to be challenged, they need to feel comfortable with hearing from us. If you only deliver negative feedback or bark orders, you'll prime people's amygdalae to heighten whenever you say anything at all. Enable people to rise to your challenges by setting a psychologically safe baseline. Ask each team member how they'd like to receive positive and constructive feedback. Kolbe Fact Finders often need some preparation. If you'd like to debrief with them over a project, consider sending them a detailed email, outlining the facts, figures, and details of your meeting agenda. After processing that, they're much more psychologically primed to receive and positively act upon your feedback. Many employees are unable to react on the fly and might need some encouraging framing language for such a conversation. Set the tone for the discussion with them by saying, "I have something difficult related to our client project together. Let's talk about it. Once we debrief, I know we'll both feel so much better." Such priming language provides clarity and reassurance.

Because most leaders and managers don't ask how their direct reports would like to receive feedback, they assume everyone likes to receive it like they do. And they often prefer a gruff, in-your-face style—either because that's all they know or because they believe such an approach projects confidence and toughness. Most people don't respond well to this style and prefer kind words and clarity about the nature of the meeting in advance. Be aware that when you ask people, some won't even be aware of how they'd like to receive feedback. But regardless of technical role, personality style, or Kolbe MO, it's often wise to use framing language and provide clarity. "Let's debrief over client X," you might say, "and discuss the highs and lows of the project. Would you take an hour and do that with me?" That response shows respect and consideration for the person and allows them to become centered and calm, instead of feeling summoned to talk about something scary. If you want the best out of your people, observe the platinum rule: do unto others as they would like done unto them.

And let's not forget: productive challenge and mentorship are required at every level of the organization, including for the CEO. Corporations have been quick to enact mentorship programs at lower rungs of the organization because talent development helps employees increase the meaning of their work and empowers them to be even greater assets to their organizations.[67] But we've all heard it's lonely at the top, and this applies to CEO development as well. Once they reach the highest leadership roles, many CEOs find that their support and mentorship networks have evaporated, as would-be advisers lack the credentials and expertise to mentor or fear negative ramifications if they provide unwelcome feedback.

But CEOs arguably are most in need of help, facing a barrage of high-stakes challenges for which they're unprepared: How do they navigate the company through a hostile takeover, a public scandal, or a stock-market crash, and how do they finesse a disagreement among the board of directors without losing the confidence of shareholders?[68] No business school seminar can prepare you for those challenges. It's no wonder that 71 percent of forty-five CEOs who'd enrolled in mentorship programs reported stronger company results: "Strong majorities reported that they were making better decisions (69%)," reported academics Suzanne de Janasz and Maury Peiperl, describing their research, "and more capably fulfilling stakeholder expectations (76%). More than anything else, these CEOs credited mentors with helping them avoid costly mistakes and become proficient in their roles faster (84%)."[69] As Chris Jones, CEO of Welsh Water, said of his mentor, "Talking these issues through with someone who has experienced similar challenges in their own past helps to give me a great deal of confidence."[70] For the good of our organizations and our larger economies, we clearly need more CEO mentors like this.

PHD SIDEBAR

DR. TRICIA'S TAKE

Bridging the gap between nature and nurture by understanding the need for **challenge**

Human beings need to be challenged in order to become better versions of themselves. When we have growth mindsets, we're able to push past our comfort zones and make ourselves vulnerable enough to pursue new skills and abilities.[71] Sure, it takes dedicated effort to make the behavioral changes necessary to push out of our comfort zones. Why does it seem that even when we expend such efforts, we can't experience such growth?

Your lazy brain gets in the way. Why don't we have growth mindsets by default? While in our comfort zones (the place where we feel safe and secure), we develop cognitive heuristics—shortcuts in our decision-making. These shortcuts are your brain's way of taking the easy road rather than expending cognitive effort to arrive at a well-structured logical analysis. Your brain wants to exert a minimal amount of effort to arrive at a decision so that it can focus its energy on other more life-sustaining tasks.

Three common types of shortcuts. Heuristics usually fall into three categories. First is representativeness (a logical leap of lumping objects or things into the same category based on known similarities). For example, if you believe that children with no siblings are lonely, and if your roommate is lonely, he must be an only child. Second is availability (determining the likelihood of an event based on personal experiences). I know an introvert who is quiet, you might think, so all introverts are quiet. Finally is satisficing (choosing the first option that meets the minimum criteria of acceptance, even if better options exist). If you've ever taken a lot of time to evaluate products in a single store, trying to choose the best bargain, instead of bargain shopping at multiple locations, then you have fallen back on a satisficing heuristic.[72] These patterns of thought can be detrimental to our growth. "No one in my family ever succeeded in school," you might observe, and reason on that basis that "I am just not meant to be good at learning." This heuristic can become so engrained that it can get applied to everything from elementary school to learning new song lyrics.

When faster thinking becomes a barrier. Your brain creates heuristics to facilitate faster decision-making.[73] These shortcuts can also serve as barriers. Heuristics operate like a "rule of thumb," allowing you to simplify situations and for this reason can be helpful. If we had to analyze every bit of information we are bombarded with every second, we might never be able to move forward. When confronting perfectionism, learning to utilize satisficing heuristics helps individuals move past analysis paralysis.[2] In most cases, individuals utilize heuristics to create protective layers around their comfort zone and decrease any chance at successful behavioral changes.

Increasing comfort with challenge begins with recognizing heuristics that represent barriers to growth. To develop a growth mindset and allow ourselves to face and overcome challenges, we first need to recognize and rewire any heuristics that suggest we avoid activities in which we are already not experts. To get a sense if heuristics are barriers to your personal growth, take a moment and reflect on any feedback you've received for needed behavioral changes or for personal growth. Write out your inner monologue about this, both positive and negative. Recognize what creates an emotional reaction, like anger, irritation, or avoidance, as this is your brain trying to keep you in your comfort zone. Find yourself an accountability partner and ask for assistance with recognizing when you are falling into this pattern. Increased awareness will help you overcome your habits and rewire your shortcuts.

Challenge yourself to determine if you are letting heuristics speak louder than facts, and if so, that's where you need to push yourself the most.

In 2018, I seized the opportunity to apply all that I'd learned from JBS and mentored a colleague. This colleague was faced with a distinct professional challenge. After her organization had hired me to coach it through the EOS model, the leader decided to sideline himself voluntarily. He was going to focus on his personal life and let others he'd been grooming assume the highest levels of leadership. This meant that she would assume his role of running the day-to-day business. Unfortunately, he found that a life away from the office wasn't as fulfilling as he'd initially thought, and after a brief hiatus away, he decided to return and assume even more control than he'd ever exercised before.

Meanwhile, my colleague had leaned into the position of organizational leader and began to experience conflict with the owner, who'd not only boomeranged back to a position of leadership but also kept inserting himself into her new role. She reminded him that he'd agreed on this direction and that the executive team was making great strides under her leadership as well. He nodded and agreed in theory but still couldn't relinquish his role in practice. Under the guise of good-heartedness and with all the best intentions, he began working at cross-purposes with her, as he continued to pursue what he believed was best for the business and all its stakeholders.

At her request, I intervened and had a meeting between these two people vying for the helm of organizational leadership. My chief objective was to achieve some alignment around both people's roles. EOS is designed to help you confront core issues like this, instead of looking for quick fixes. Unfortunately, alignment wasn't to be achieved: the owner insisted on taking charge of the business and was unwilling to compromise. For her part, she was ready for the challenge of leadership and not content taking a back seat to the owner. In December of 2019, she made the difficult choice to leave the organization.

She reached out to me through this process, and among the advice I gave her was to start a journal, recording her thoughts, reflections, and ideas for different growth possibilities outside of this organization. Therapists and mental health experts have long extolled the power of journaling, and it didn't disappoint in her case. She experienced many epiphanies and "aha!" moments as she reflected on her journey at the organization. Journaling proved so critical because she couldn't talk to her coworkers, direct reports, or even her husband about what was going on. They just couldn't understand. Instead, she needed to dialogue with herself and gain clarity on what she wanted in a business role. Some leaders, she realized, were meant to lead together forever, while others were destined to colead for a season and then assume different destines apart.

Our mentorship calls also focused on her many strengths. In particular, I was always struck by how quickly she took to the EOS framework I'd introduced at the company. The system immediately resonated with her, and she'd guided others through it, helping to realign the organization along more human-centered needs in the process. So one day during our call, I asked her bluntly, "Have you ever considered capitalizing on your strengths and becoming a business coach?"

My question was shocking—terrorizing even! The stakes were high. She'd been successful throughout her career but now had reached a major pivot, or personal/professional inflection point. She was about to turn fifty and had only served in three positions. Though these were all elevated leadership positions, she'd never envisaged herself as acting in an entrepreneurial capacity like I did, owning and directing her own company and thereby exercising leadership in a much different capacity. "I was perfectly OK being a CEO for someone else's company and acting as an owner without equity," she reflected on a call with me. Could she actually perform this much different role? I reminded her that what looked like a daunting change might not be: she'd been able to mentor others within her organization and significantly improve their performance. I expressed confidence in her, just like JBS had in me.

Since she was a Kolbe initiating Fact Finder, this move was an unknown and therefore entailed a great deal of risk. You might even call this the definitive challenge of her life. But because of this period of introspective journaling and mentorship with me, she was able to recognize the gifts she possessed and the great potential this new opportunity entailed. This in turn enabled her to transcend her human instinct to just focus on the risk and instead usher in the great possibilities it entailed for her and her future clients. Without too much thought, she decided to do it. In January of 2019, she became a business coach.

"This was the riskiest thing I've ever done in my entire life. And I'm not a risk-taker!" she reflected.

But since making the decision, she's never looked back. I've continued to serve as her mentor ever since. You've probably noticed that my style is naturally different than JBS's, and she needed something a little different than I had experienced with him. When it comes to my mentorship with her, I never give advice and apply pressure and instead pose question and plant seeds, motivating her to come to her own conclusions and devise her own solutions. I know that she needed this style of mentorship because we'd discussed what she needed in a mentor. "When mentoring me," she described, "and getting me to go from good to great and from great to better, I need to be in the driver's seat."

But though I never push her to make decisions, I'm always nudging her to improvement. We speak about twice a month together on our "Monday kick-butt" calls, when we discuss her progress and how we can challenge her business to new growth and possibilities. She's so intrinsically motivated to improve that it's a pleasure guiding her—and pushing her. In early 2020, I invited her to a conference called Wise Women. I alerted her that a spot was open and that she'd be ideal. She expressed immediate reservations: "I don't know if I'm wise enough." But I challenged her right back, telling her there was a lot she could contribute and that she'd certainly derive value from the experience. She trusted me and attended—predictably, it was great.

We'd reached that ideal spot in the coaching relationship in which she trusted me to calibrate the challenge to what she needed. That's always the trick when it comes to challenging others—even ourselves. Our challenges must be productive—difficult but not so overwhelming that we withdraw if we fall short. She's now opened her own business and hired an assistant. This young woman is trying to become an entrepreneur herself, and she is now paying all she's learned forward, mentoring this young person to stand on her own and see the potential in herself. From JBS to me to my colleague and now my colleague's assistant—we've created a virtuous cycle of productive mentorship, challenging others in our lives to new heights.

Buddha is rumored to have said, "When the student is ready, the teacher will appear." Whether he said it or not, it's perennially true and relevant. I've always been struck at how, in such uncanny ways, different mentors, coaches, and authority figures have appeared in my life precisely at the moments I needed them. JBS is one example, and I'm gratified that he enabled me to supply my executive leadership coaching to even more businesses in this country. He also modeled how to proactively seek out individual mentees. But when it comes to mentorship, more is "caught, not taught." No matter who you are, you can challenge everyone around you to be better, stronger, and kinder simply by modeling this conduct in the workplace and in your personal life. I find this form of unofficial mentorship, manifest in small challenges we model to others, to be extremely effective and inspiring. If we do this as leaders and managers, this behavior can become part of a larger culture of self-improvement and integrity. If we do this as spouses, parents, and community leaders, we can create positive ripples throughout our world.

Of course, we must also be careful to provide *healthy* challenges. In the case of my experience with Bill's team, the challenge I was initially presented—to seed, scale, and help market a company that could effect change in the market—had morphed into an unhealthy challenge. Instead of a healthy business purpose, my challenge was to navigate interpersonal land mines, which was not only unproductive but was damaging to me and everyone else.

As leaders and managers, we have a special responsibility to productively challenge our team members through modeling the qualities we seek to see in our cultures and via traditional mentorship relationships. Think about ways you can challenge your direct reports and team members by holding them accountable and thereby helping them reach new heights of performance and transformation.

Dustin Bankston, the sales and estimating manager at Jewett Roofing, didn't always recognize the human requirement for challenge. He's been a tradesman since he was an adolescent, working after school and during summers to hone his craft. After graduation, he began working full time in the roofing industry. He started in the residential sector, working his way into bigger and more complicated commercial and industrial roofing projects.

"When I started at Jewett," Dustin recalled, "I was a grunt. Low man on the totem pole." In addition to swinging a hammer and installing roofing material, he pushed wheelbarrows and was assigned the downright dirty work that no senior crew member wanted to perform. Roofers typically work in teams of four to eight people, and Dustin came to enjoy the camaraderie that developed when teams had a great leader—one that inspired everyone to consistently show up and gel with one another. It's especially important when installing a roof on a crew—everyone needs to operate machinery efficiently and move about freely and in sync with others instead of focusing on people's quirks and flaws. A few bad apples, and entire projects—not to mention personal safety—risk being compromised.

Construction sites are constant, unending sources of challenge. These range from too much heat and humidity to overcoming mental and physical fatigue, equipment problems, and handling material delays. Luckily, Dustin's experience navigating these challenges gradually paid off as he worked his way up the pecking order to lead foreman, even venturing into operations. But then a job in sales came up in 2013, and Dan Jewett, the company owner, encouraged Dustin to apply.

It seemed like a good fit. Dustin loves talking to people and determining what makes them tick—an excellent trait for a salesman. The owner, in turn, likes promoting in-house and saw something special and promising in Dustin. Dustin began shadowing Bob, the company's veteran sales manager, studying his methods in context and familiarizing himself with this entirely new facet of the construction business. Dustin had come a long way from hauling wheelbarrows and dirty work!

He felt ready for this new challenge—until his first presentation, that is. For his inaugural pitch, Dustin prepared a presentation for a church near Springfield, Illinois, that needed a new roof. Jewett doesn't email quotes, preferring instead to meet in person during a bidding round, walking potential clients through the process and explaining the pricing in detail. Dustin therefore presented to one of the church's board members, with his sales manager at his side. "It wasn't like I was in front of ten people," Dustin remembers, "but I was worked up and was so nervous."

Dustin is probably being a little too self-critical when he

says that. After all, he was drawing from an entirely different set of skills than he'd diligently spent his life honing. He had to pivot from a tradesman to a salesman, and that wasn't easy. He worked himself into a frenzy during his presentation, mincing his words and sweating profusely. Seeing everything derail, Bob took Dustin aside and told him to take a few breaths and calm himself. "We've rehearsed this," he reminded Dustin; "you know exactly what to do." But he lacked confidence in his abilities, and his anxiety overcame him. "I'm just a roofer," he thought. "I'm no one special"—definitely not a cocky sales guy. The church decided to go with another company.

After that setback, Dustin could have shrunk away from the challenge and returned to the nuts and bolts of roofing— his undisputed core specialty. But he pressed on instead, doing more presentations. Each one he did, the easier it became. And now, it's the most exciting part of the whole sales process. In fact, it's his favorite part of his whole job! He looks forward to walking large groups of potential clients through the roofing process. And he's found that most clients don't want a cocky sales guy in front of them anyway. This approach works for some people, but it wasn't Dustin's style. And part of Dustin leaning into this challenge was drawing on his professional background and distinct personality traits to determine the most effective style for him. He found that potential clients responded best when they experienced Dustin's history and skill set in roofing. Instead of selling them flashy products, Dustin assumes a contractor's approach, asking targeted questions, seeking to discern where problems are and providing professional solutions for them, and ensuring that potential clients understand everything about the product and solution they are buying. After all, sometimes clients are asked to spend vast sums of money on a roof, something they'll never even see.

Dustin understands how vital a need that challenge is

in work. Without being given this immense professional challenge in sales, he would never have experienced the job satisfaction, energy, enthusiasm, and confidence that comes from his expanded skill set. And if he ever feels nervous or intimidated before a big presentation, he remembers that first bid for the church and how far he's come since then. Not only is he more competent now, but he's gone from pitching $20,000 projects to $500,000 ones and counting. That's always the confidence booster he needs. But it's also humbling, as he's reminded that it's the confident tradesman with a career's worth of expertise, and not a flashy salesman, that accounts for his success. As the jobs get pricier, the risks get higher too. But that's all right: Dustin is up for the challenge!

As you consider how to help your organization fulfill this human need of challenge, consider the following questions:

1. Is the group size three to seven people?

2. How do you or will you handle collaboration and conflict?

3. What is the current trust level on the team? (1–10)

4. Do you have a coaching and/or mentoring program or process?

5. Do you have tools in place to review and analyze team performance?

6. Do we have a systematic way to ensure continuous improvement?

SIX FACETS *of* HUMAN NEEDS

CONFIDENCE · CLARITY · CONNECTION · CONTRIBUTION · CHALLENGE · CONSIDERATION

CHAPTER 7
Consideration

"Labor is prior to, and independent of, capital. Capital is only the fruit of labor and could never have existed if labor had not first existed. Labor is the superior of capital and deserves much the higher consideration."

—ABRAHAM LINCOLN

D o you remember learning about stars in high school astronomy class? Let me give you something even better than you learned in school: the astronomy of business. As leaders and managers, we all have bright, shining stars in our "solar systems" (businesses or teams) that we want to nurture, engage, and retain. Sometimes we cultivate this talent properly, and our stars shine bright, illuminating and enriching entire galaxies (business ecosystems or industries). Oftentimes we neglect these star players, and instead of helping them to shine even brighter, we dampen their illumination, transforming them into dimming stars—disengaging and becoming complacent. Sometimes complacency settles in, and they become falling stars; other times they become shooting stars, leaving your galaxy for somewhere more hospitable. When such exiting stars depart, they can leave a trail of destruction in their wake.

BUSINESS ASTRONOMY

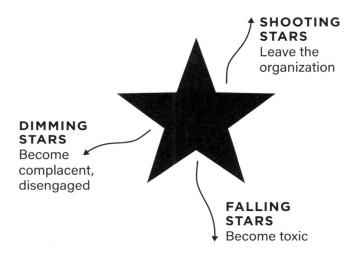

SHOOTING STARS
Leave the organization

DIMMING STARS
Become complacent, disengaged

FALLING STARS
Become toxic

Throughout this book, I've recounted my experiences in several of these "stellar" situations. During one bout of workplace toxicity, when I lacked clarity about my role (not to mention baseline consideration), I dimmed my star. It was a self-protective move I made in a hostile environment, in which no one seemed to care or appreciate my brightness. Of course, I was given the perfunctory fruit basket and plastered-on smile, but I saw this for what it was: fake, ungenuine consideration. Later on, I became a shooting star and created my own solar system, where I could shine brightly.

Falling stars are even rarer but more dangerous, as they become toxic to the organization by falling into bad behaviors and derailing culture. Shooting stars leave the organization. These shooting stars were once model employees. Hardened from periods of neglect and lack of recognition, however, they leave and sometimes decide to punish the organization as they go. Sometimes you'll even have a boomeranging star, like Steve Jobs, who was forced out of his organization only be called back in, the new stars unable to appropriately and effectively illuminate the organization without him.

All too often, I see leaders and managers respond to dimming, falling, or shooting stars with grand gestures, offering bonuses, enhanced compensation plans, and stock options to retain their talent. And while it's nice to get extra money and financial perks, that won't keep a star in your company orbit. Think about Maslow's hierarchy of needs—these financial incentives represent the lowest rung on the hierarchy, satisfying basic security. When it comes to retaining our stars and helping them shine on our teams and organizations, noncash incentives ranging from high fives to handwritten notes to elaborate displays of appreciation will go a lot further than this.

After all, we've all experienced that special feeling of consideration—appreciation, respect, and high regard. We've all felt like brightly lit stars at home and at work, and it was wonderful. That's because we all have a human need to be recognized and valued; when that feeling is fulfilled, something deep within us is fulfilled.

Unfortunately, we probably have more memories of the opposite feeling. Have you ever expended significant effort at work, confronted major challenges, made important contributions to your team, and then wondered, "Does anyone even care?" Guess what? The lack of recognition and thanks means one of your fundamental needs is going unaddressed. This human need comes toward the end of the journey through the 6 Cs, but it's just as vital as the others. Even if you have clarity on your role, are connected to a team or mission, and achieve healthy levels of challenge and contribution, this need still lingers, often unaddressed.

You've probably heard the expression "People don't care how much you know until they know how much you care." I've heard this all my life, but when I went to Google to determine its origin, I found it attributed to a bewildering number of people, as diverse as Theodor Roosevelt and Earl Nightingale. These individuals probably did say this phrase at some point because it speaks to common human need. We've all been in those one-way conversations where people were talking at us instead of with us. In those interactions, we feel slighted and insulted because the person doesn't care about us enough to even *consider* our responses. Instead we serve as sounding boards, as the person waits for us to stop talking so that they can begin again. High performance and human thriving can't exist in this one-sided environment. We can't have successful teams and organizations if we don't recognize and consider every member on it.

Unfortunately, leaders and managers often spend their time and attention—their consideration—on the wrong people. We waste time on toxic or poor-performing people and not enough time showing consideration for our stars. Our stars are often diligently at work on their projects and teams, and when a new committee or project position becomes available, they're disappointed when someone else is appointed. "I'm not even being *considered* for these promotions," the person often thinks, "even though I'm doing everything right." You can't obtain and retain top talent if you don't show them respect and consideration at every stage of the journey. They must be recognized for good work, thought about for promotions, and reminded of how critical they are to the organization. Or they'll leave and satisfy this human need at a different company.

CONSIDERATION MOTIVATES PERFORMANCE

When I was a web business developer at the turn of the century, I learned an important lesson about human consideration. This was during the most tumultuous and high-performance part of my career, which I described in chapter 1. I managed a small team, had some direct reports, and was a project facilitator for what would become "digital" years later. American Express had merged with a new venture, and I was bridging the gap between the new venture's company's technology and marketing teams, creating an online presence for our incentive card—what would eventually become the world's first gift card. Two different corporate teams of a hundred people from New York and St. Louis, all with different cultures and different policies and procedures, were merging.

We were moving into new office space, collaborating on the launch of multiple internet sites and website applications. And we had to accomplish all this on a compressed timetable. The internet was new, and no one knew if they went online to check their card balances whether their information would be tampered with. We didn't even have our offices set up or our corporate logos ready. But we were launching websites. It was a high-risk, high-innovation time, and the tempo of my teams was "go, go, go." And I can't emphasize enough how much work everyone expended.

Instead of stopping to say "hey, thanks" or to give a high five (this was the 1990s, and the "fist bump" was yet to become popular, let alone the post-COVID "namaste bow" or "elbow bump"), we just moved furiously from one project to another. One of my managers took notice and ushered me aside one day and said, "Your team loves you, and you're doing a great job. Everyone's energized by this work and is contributing to make great things happen."

"So what's the problem?" I asked.

"You're going to burn them out."

It was my first time managing people, and I clearly didn't understand one of the most important parts of people management: consideration. I'd led this group of excellent high performers through war and left them unappreciated. If I kept this up, I might lose them. I paused for a moment after that sobering feedback. It was about thirty to forty-five days into this push, and my team was slowly dimming. They were starting to miss small deadlines and expend less energy during our meetings.

I changed course and every Wednesday dedicated fifteen minutes to my project teams, direct reports, and my coworkers, focusing on the gratitude and appreciation I had for them and all they'd accomplished that past week. I didn't recognize everyone each week—that would cheapen my gestures. Instead, I seized on anything that came to mind, anything that was special and noteworthy, and I recognized it with handwritten notes or high-fiving. Even if someone was just walking by on the hall, I'd raise my voice and say, "Hey, that suggestion you made last week during the meeting—major game changer! Thanks so much. Well done!"

At first, the difference in the team was subtle. Everyone sat up a little taller and almost responded bashfully to my praise (*"Really, you saw that?"*). With minimal effort, I'd taken this group of high performers and instilled team intimacy and trust for the organization. I'd let them know that amid all the corporate change and activity, they could feel good about their projects and teams. I'd proven a time-honored military aphorism true. On the battleground, Napoleon is rumored to have said, "A soldier will fight long and hard for a piece of colored ribbon."[74]

This declaration has been misconstrued to mean that leaders can manipulate their direct reports, even get them to willingly sacrifice their lives, if they get some silly recognition. Some might say it's in line with generational thinking—the "everyone should get a trophy" mentality of recognizing everyone merely for participating instead of achieving. But I don't believe that's the essence of the quote. We can inspire our soldiers to greatness, Napoleon seems to say, if we provide them with genuine recognition for their contribution. And it proved true in my case. After I'd doled out some appropriate, targeted ribbon, the energy on my teams elevated, as did my high productivity rates and general morale. My flagging teams perked right back up, everyone adhered to small deadlines, and there was more smiling and laughter throughout the workplace.

In thinking further about consideration, I turned to the company's core value of "work hard, have fun." We'd nailed the first part, I realized, but we'd neglected the second. We started to celebrate big launch hits with lunches or with end-of-day champagne toasts. We'd uncork a bottle of champagne and everyone would smile, ready to toast our hard work with some levity. I don't want to take too much credit here. There many factors that contributed to our team synergy, and I was by no means the epicenter. But I do believe that my small acts of consideration catalyzed a change in our larger team culture. And that in turn helped us make our goal: by April 1, our teams were integrated, our offices were unpacked, and we'd launched an improbable array of internet activities and initiatives. There wasn't a single deadline or business goal we missed, and we all felt gratified by what we'd accomplished together.

DR. TRICIA'S TAKE

Bridging the gap between nature and nurture by understanding the need for **consideration**

Human beings have a basic need for consideration: to be held in regard and feel appreciated. It feels good to be recognized and appreciated, and lacking that feeling is often determinantal to an individual's self-worth and ability to perform.

SELF-ESTEEM AND WHY IT MATTERS

As adults in working environments, there are several reasons why we need consideration, including having our own self-worth mirrored back to us through others.[75] During our formative years of development, we rely on signals from others to tell us if we are doing well, and we internalize those signals as a measure of our own self-worth. When human beings feel seen, heard, acknowledged, and appreciated, their self-esteem increases. Self-esteem is an essential and vital component of the human experience, with several studies correlating positive self-esteem with overall well-being.[76]

CONSIDERATION AND COUNTERPRODUCTIVE WORK BEHAVIORS

From an evolutionary perspective, it makes sense that human beings feel a desire for teaming (i.e., joining in cooperative efforts). Teaming increases the odds of survival. When individuals don't feel valued by the team, negativity might outweigh the good. When individuals feel a lack of consideration, they will likely disengage. Disengagement can bring many organizational problems, like counterproductive work behaviors

(CWBs).[77] CWBs are intentional actions that can range from passive-aggressive behavior (e.g., intentionally slowing the pace of work output) to illegal and dangerous actions (e.g., stealing company property or exposing a teammate to a known food allergy). CWBs are hard to quantify because they entail a wide range of behaviors and because not everyone will cop to committing such behaviors. However, one study found that up to 89 percent of employees engage in some form of CWBs, ranging from more mild (e.g., gossiping) to more extreme (e.g., bullying or even physical violence).[78] Teams with a history of lack of consideration for one another not only lack trust, but they also are also more likely to suffer from CWBs.

Consideration is more than just being nice. Team interaction should be designed and structured to increase individual self-esteem and reduce CWBs. Often teams underestimate their impact in this area. Even in the highest-functioning teams, I've observed (in my own work) a pattern of accepting destructive behavior on teams. This encompasses active forms, like negative nicknames or running jokes at an individual's expense, and passive forms, like when a subgroup meets after a meeting to discuss how irritating they found a team member's behavior, keeping the offending team member in the dark. These behaviors, large or small, erode a team over time.

To develop a foundation of consideration on a team, begin by considering each individual's preference for recognition. Some enjoy the limelight, while others actively avoid it. Use something like the "love languages" assessment, discussed in this book, to individualize consideration and achieve organizational health and performance.[79]

Harness the power of consideration through developing

meaningful recognition on your team. There are many ways to do this, whether formally or informally, and you can shape your recognition programs based on what is truly meaningful to your team. Recognition can be based on more traditional factors with award programs based on length of tenure in the organization (this is usually done in increments like one, five, or ten years of service) or bonus structure based on hitting or exceeding key performance indicators on a project. Alternatively, your team may value more unique forms of celebration, like a quarterly award for most positive impact on team morale or awarding badges to team members who outwardly express team or organizational values. The key is to ensure that recognition is intentionally developed. Do not just adopt something without thought. Meaningful recognition works; surface-level practices do not.

INCENTIVE OR NOT? THAT IS THE QUESTION

We all want our teams to function as optimally as mine in the 1990s did. And our businesses and business scholars have worked hard to determine how best to motivate and engage workers. In 1993, the *Harvard Business Review* published a debate about workforce motivation that resonates to today. Evaluating scholars, workplaces, laboratories, and similar settings, scholar Alfie Kohn noted the universality of financial incentive programs. But he was convinced that offering incentives, just like applying punishments, was "strikingly ineffective," guaranteeing "temporary compliance" at best, or even counterproductive results at worst.[80] That's because whether the incentive was a cash bonus or a heartily administered pat on the back, it represented an extrinsic source of motivation. Just like seat belts, cigarettes, and weight loss—once the incentives to modify one's lifestyle disappear, so does the behavior (and oftentimes it's worse than if no incentives had been ever offered). "Rewards do not create a lasting commitment. They merely, and temporarily, change what we do," Kohn suggested.[81] That makes incentives pernicious—bribes and quid pro quos that inhibit risk-taking, creativity, exploration, and innovation.

A group of business scholars responded to Kohn that year in the same publication, all crying nonsense! Bribes are not the same as fair compensation for a job well done. According to the studies they analyzed, workers needed to be intrinsically motivated. But extrinsic rewards are some nice icing to the professional cake—they can motivate extra creativity and innovation when judiciously applied.[82] According to businessman and article coauthor Jerry McAdams, "Appropriate rewards for improved performance have always made good sense, intuitively and practically. They aren't wrong. They aren't intrinsically demotivating."[83] These authors suggest that extrinsic and intrinsic rewards can positively reinforce one another in a virtuous cycle. Famed poet Anne Sexton perhaps said it best: "I am in love with money, so don't be mistaken. But first I want to write good poems. After that, I am anxious as hell to earn money and fame and bring the stars all down."[84]

Since the late twentieth century, we've reframed the debate slightly, but corporate incentive programs haven't dramatically changed. We're still debating the merits of intrinsic versus extrinsic motivation, and if we've spent any time in the corporate world, we've likely experienced how ineffective most incentive programs are.[85] But many companies have since come to engage employees by progressively addressing the human need of consideration. In 1993, for example, the United States passed the Family and Medical Leave Act, allowing for paid maternal leave after a pregnancy or guaranteed compensation if workers become sick or have to care for a distressed family member. Workforces also took bold steps to diversify their ranks, ensuring that historically disadvantaged minorities, women, and other groups would be considered during hiring and promotion. And since that time, companies have embraced noncash incentives, retaining top talent through providing on-site childcare, flexible work hours to accommodate parental obligations, and personal leadership and training programs. They've even offered virtual media and paycheck protection to help people return to work after external threats like the COVID-19 pandemic.

Much has been made of Silicon Valley's famously "considerate" workplaces, where employees are given freedom to dress in flip-flops and hoodies and break up their days with ping-pong matches and round-the-clock catered food. But I prefer less flashy, more public shows of consideration at these same companies, especially when they creatively address their workforces' human needs. Lazlo Bock, Google's senior vice president of people, introduced a peer recognition tool called gThanks, allowing team members to publicly share "kudos" when their teammates do well and to further publicize them on Google+.[86] Its creator believes that this is infinitely superior to a private recognition of accomplishment or a cash incentive because they are shrouded in secrecy. Instead, this public display of recognition is highly motivating—especially since Bock printed the gThanks notes and displayed them outside his office. "Simple, public recognition is one of the most effective and most underutilized management tools," affirmed Bock.[87] I couldn't agree more because such recognition addresses the workplace need of consideration.

Whether you have an incentive program or a personal policy of showing appreciation for the people on your team, make sure it is authentic, consistent, and aligned with other behavior. My former mentor and boss interspersing his tirades with the occasional fruit basket is the perfect example; because the environment was toxic and the needs of the team were not being considered, let alone met, any consideration I received felt false and reeked of inauthenticity.

One of my favorite frameworks for manifesting consideration is *The 5 Languages of Appreciation in the Workplace*. You might not have heard of this book, but perhaps you are familiar with Gary Chapman's runaway best seller about the five love languages. If you didn't, here's a quick synopsis. In relationships, Chapman discovered five different orientations or "languages" that we naturally prefer or to which we naturally gravitate: quality time, words of affirmation, receiving gifts, physical touch, and acts of service. Unfortunately, we tend to speak the love language that we like to others—big mistake! The trick to a successful relationship, per Chapman, is to learn our partner's love language and use it to speak to them. Couples the world over have raved about how this simple change has revolutionized their marriages and happiness together.

> **Whether you have an incentive program or a personal policy of showing appreciation for the people on your team, make sure it is authentic, consistent, and aligned with other behavior.**

Luckily, Chapman adapted the five love languages to the workplace as well, and it works just as well.[88] Think about it: we are all in long-term committed relationships with our coworkers and customers. Wouldn't it be great to think about the way they like to be appreciated and respond to them in kind? If your love language is giving gifts, we know that flowers and chocolates might not be appropriate in work settings. But we can take a broad interpretation of gifts in the workplace—anything from a gThanks shout-out, if you work at Google, or perhaps a personalized note. Maybe someone on your team is a die-hard yoga fanatic, and perhaps you read an interesting profile in the morning paper on the topic. Cut it out and or send it via email to the person to show you were thinking of them—I guarantee that this thoughtful gesture will speak volumes and make your colleague feel appreciated.

Perhaps your love language is quality time—there's nothing you appreciate more or that bonds you to others more than time well spent with others. If you know that about your direct report or an important customer, then you can respond in turn, creating a corporate culture that celebrates milestones with champagne toasts and ushers in the holidays with festivities. If someone on your team thrives on quality time, you might expend some extra energy to debrief after big projects or plan a lunch for their performance review, taking time to talk them through their accomplishment and growth areas.

Perhaps the most controversial love language in the workplace is physical touch. I'm sure the image of touching our colleagues conjures dread, whether we fear spreading disease (after the COVID-19 pandemic) or misinterpretation of such gestures as sexual harassment. I won't lie—this is probably the most difficult love language to translate into a work setting, especially given that different cultures have different degrees of physical intimacy (some cultures take bows, some kiss on the lips). Give this one some thought. There's nothing wrong with an elbow bump or an innocent pat on the shoulder when this is the way that our colleagues like appreciation.

Acts of service and words of affirmation, by contrast, are easy to translate into a business setting. As I've shared, thoughtful words affirming great conduct and performance are invaluable—and when this is a coworker's love language, they probably mean more than cash bonuses or other perks. Shoot off a Slack message or email to your coworker and tell them how they shined on a project—or better yet, a handcrafted thank-you note of recognition. Acts of service are a wonderful way to show appreciation for the time and feelings of others—whether its reviewing a big project or taking a shift when someone needs personal time or even volunteering to take something off a struggling or overwhelmed colleague's plate.

One of the many advantages of *The 5 Languages of Appreciation in the Workplace* is that it's premised on the platinum rule. Let me explain by way of example. Executive coach CJ McClanahan loves books.[89] The man doesn't golf or collect figurines or spend his time dancing. He's a man who loves the written word. Whenever Christmas, birthdays, or major events arose, he naturally gifted his loved ones with—you guessed it—a book. What he found, of course, was that his friends and family had accumulated a bunch of unread books in their homes. McClanahan's heart was in the right spot, but he'd committed the sin of self-obsession. And that's easy to do. As he relates:

> We're all a little guilty of assuming that everyone has the same interests/desires/passions as we do. It's pervasive throughout society. As a leader, we assume that our direct reports want a similar career path filled with promotions, responsibilities and a bigger salary. We assume our friends like to do the same things, watch similar shows on TV and have the same expectations for their kids. Our schools are built on the premise that every kid learns the same way and they should all go to a four-year college.[90]

The only way to overcome this natural tendency is to embrace the platinum rule: do unto others as *they* would like done unto them. It takes us away from focusing on ourselves and to considering

133

others. If we embrace the platinum rule, consider the uniqueness of others, and even try things like the five languages of appreciation in the workplace, we'll create workplaces that fulfill the human need of consideration.

* * *

We began the chapter with a business astronomy analogy, and so it's fitting we end there as well, returning to our discussion of stars. As we know, sometimes when we don't treat our stars well, they'll fall or shoot away. Sometimes, however, something trickier and more difficult to detect occurs. Certain star performers begin to brown out, just like dying stars. According to Michael Kibler, an expert on this topic, don't mistake them for dimming stars: "Brownout is different from burnout because workers afflicted by it are not in obvious crisis," Kibler said. "They seem to be performing fine: putting in massive hours, grinding out work while contributing to teams, and saying all the right things in meetings. However, they are operating in a silent state of continual overwhelm, and the predictable consequence is disengagement."[91]

That's right: you'll mistake these stars for being happy and content, until they take their expertise and passion right out of your company. According to Kibler, you won't get anywhere by throwing money and incentives at these dimming stars—it'll either provide them more motivation to leave or keep them at the company in their dissatisfied condition.[92] Instead, he advises offering them something akin to consideration.

When it comes to preventing death by brownout in your top stars, Kibler suggests partnering with these stars on personal or professional goals. Engage in frank conversations with these people and help them identify and address goals: maybe they want to become more physically fit, start a not-for-profit organization, volunteer in the community, build more robust relationships with clients, or take on a challenge at the business.[93] "When firms do [this]," Kibler suggests, "it dramatically increases the commitment and impact of its stars." And if you are skeptical of this as a way to reduce brownout, then just look at the Big 4 Professional service organizations or other elite organizations—chances are they have already implemented these executive programs. And that's why they are winning the global war on talent. You can do the same—the key is to address human consideration.

Tina Lynn, a certified veterinary technician, has always been very considerate, especially when it comes to animals. Since deciding to pursue a veterinary technician program, she's loved every day of her work.

Not that it's easy. Originally, she worked in an emergency medicine context at night. It was just her and the veterinarian helping distressed animals, sometimes at two in the morning. She worked with over twenty different veterinarians during that time and learned how to handle different personalities and work styles. Now, having transferred to a daytime practice, she's slowly come to enjoy serving on teams larger than two and appreciates an extra person to cover her up front as she's working with a patient in the back office.

The constant challenges of veterinary medicine filled her with purpose and meaning that have only increased as she's progressed in her career. In emergency medicine, you rarely know a patient's ultimate outcome—they only visit when distressed. In the daytime practice she enjoys now, she finds herself spending more time learning about and developing relationships with her clients and their pets, enjoying profound bonds that develop over time. The more she and her clients have gotten to know one another, the more everyone relies on Tina. A common refrain at the practice: "I'm going to ask Tina—she'll know what to do." Tina seems to have everything: clarity of role, connection to others, contributing to a noble but challenging mission, and confidence she can discharge her role. There's only one item missing.

One of the primary owners of the veterinary practice where she now works has an unyielding, my-way-or-the-highway attitude. When Tina began at the company, the entire practice was small—probably five employees in total—and everyone adjusted to him, walking on eggshells as they navigated his moods. By 2019, the company had grown to over thirty-five employees and three locations. Tina was now on the leadership team and in charge of hiring and found herself sitting across the table from talented potential employees, trying to lure them by sharing the company's core values. She found herself increasingly ill at ease and compromised, lying to people by omission because she didn't tell them about the owner and his temperament.

Finally, after considerable reflection, she decided to be courageous and share her feelings. She had to do it because, in her words, "the lack of consideration this owner showed the staff" had reached a breaking point. Case in point: Tina had worked every Saturday for six months and had never been acknowledged for it. Not a single "thank you," "good job," or offer to give her a weekend off.

"I felt very unappreciated," she recalls. She'd willfully chosen to sacrifice, of course, knowing the company was short-staffed. But then her goodwill was taken advantage of and began rapidly declining. One Saturday, the owner sent a friend to the clinic ten minutes prior to closing for an examination. He autonomically assumed that Tina would work overtime on the weekend to help with his friend's pet. "It hit me," Tina recalled. "My time was not as valuable as his."

Perhaps even more distressing was his treatment of others. Christy, a talented customer service representative at the clinic, radiates personality. She's so considerate and hardworking that everyone values her immensely. One day, as she was navigating the clinic, getting everything done, the owner muttered under his breath, "Somebody needs to sedate her." How could he possibly say something so insulting for someone bending over backward for his company? Tina thought.

Tina realized she wasn't on the right team anymore and that she couldn't sit across the table from potential recruits and encourage them to come on board. That would be inconsiderate (and unethical). Absent a drastic change, she couldn't continue working for the company. She shared these thoughts with the leadership and was shocked and flattered to see how much everyone valued her as a team member. One veterinarian was on her doorstep within twenty minutes of her posting her note online, asking how he could help. Her phone rang off the hook with people singing her praises and trying to convince her to stay. After five days, the owner sent a letter of apology, and the group decided that Tina would take a leave of absence until the company's quarterly meeting with me. When I conducted the off-site team meeting, everyone was extremely honest and cooperative.

One of the reasons I'm optimistic about this veterinary practice is that there are pockets of consideration elsewhere at the company. For example, Tina meets quarterly with her colleagues and discusses customer care, patient care, scheduling, and other such matters. These check-ins are powerful for Tina, because everyone can debrief and reflect on the practice's operations as a team. She also meets in subgroups every few weeks or so to ensure operations are running smoothly.

Now sprawling across three campuses, each about twenty miles apart, the practice is more complex. Tina's location has a little bit of an older and lower-income clientele. At one of the quarterly meetings, Tina suggested that if her location adjusted its rates to accommodate this clientele's needs, they'd do better financially. And guess what? Her location is more profitable than the others. Consideration is clearly something that applies to individuals, teams, companies, and stakeholders. When Tina considered the particular needs of her clientele, everyone benefited. Tina has taught me that mutual consideration builds morale, creates happy customers, and helps drive profitability.

At the beginning of her career, Tina didn't think one way or another about consideration. But she now knows that human consideration is a vital workplace need. Without it, Tina says, you'll have businesses filled with employees clocking in and clocking out, without larger purpose, mission, and dedication. Lacking that is particularly dangerous in the care professions. Tina has certainly shown me how consideration works operationally, and interpersonally, and how it's a critical linchpin in either reinforcing or undermining company values. I sincerely hope that the lack of consideration emanating from the highest levels of veterinary leadership can change so that this practice can remain vibrant, profitable, and healthy in the long term. The fate of many people, including Tina and important furry members of the community, hangs in the balance.

Six questions to meet the need of consideration:

1. Have you blocked your calendar to make time for appreciation and gratitude?

2. Do rewards, incentives, and recognition programs drive the results you want to see? Are they producing counterproductive results and outcomes?

3. Do you know each direct report's "story" in order to know them as a "whole person" (personal, professional, cognitive, affective, conative, etc.)?

4. Do you have regular and scheduled one-on-one meetings to allow for listening so that they are heard and all perspectives are considered?

5. Do you know the "language of appreciation" that each member on your team prefers?

6. Are you available to all team members on a regular basis? Do you make time to walk around the operations area of the business—making yourself present?

SIX
FACETS
of
HUMAN
NEEDS

CONFIDENCE   CLARITY   CONSIDERATION   CONNECTION   CHALLENGE   CONTRIBUTION

CHAPTER 8
Confidence

"Confidence is going after Moby Dick in a
rowboat and taking tartar sauce with you."

—ZIG ZIGLAR

t the beginning of 2020, as I was writing this book, the sky fell. Metaphorically speaking. After ten years of staggering and dazzling growth across the developed world, a highly contagious virus began silently circulating the globe, threatening to upend all of this prosperity and progress. Health experts suggest that it began in China, and thanks to our globalized world, soon it came to engulf the rest of the globe, most of which responded in an unprecedented fashion: voluntarily shutting down the economy to mitigate the spread of the disease. Businesses shuttered their doors, sending markets into turmoil, and entire industries halted to a standstill, sending supply chains into disarray and millions to their local unemployment offices. Whatever else we may say about this virus, this is for certain: it caused a massive crisis in confidence.

As the novel coronavirus shocked the world, there was very little encouragement I could offer my clients. We were all on a roller coaster, unable to predict how the virus would infect others, and how the economic fallout would ultimately affect our businesses. So instead of offering predictions or circulating trite but well-meaning memes that "everything will work out," I sent my clients an encouraging article from the *Harvard Business Review.*[94]

It was nearing mid-March of 2020, and according to these authors, all in management roles affiliated with the Boston Consulting Group and all experts on Chinese businesses and economic recovery, China was beginning to recover economically. The Chinese companies that had reviewed market dynamics and reacted accordingly were already improving. Noodle and drink company Master Kong, for example, pivoted away from its traditional customers and shifted to e-commerce and smaller retail outlets. It remained nimble and flexible, making its supply chain able to improve by over half, and supply threefold the amount of supplies than its competitors.

The authors cited more proof of companies that had helped create clarity for employees and stakeholders, through apps, internal platforms, social media, and spontaneous and even preventative health checkups; some shifted employees from, say, serving customers food to planning for the recovery process and had improved in turn. "Only six weeks after the initial outbreak," the authors observe, "China appears to be in the early stages of recovery ... And confidence appears to be coming back as seen in real estate transactions, which had fallen to 1% of 2019 levels but have since bounced back to 47%."[95]

I'm not at all suggesting that this article was definitive or that there aren't myriad complexities to China and the rest of the world's recovery from the disease and its economic fallout. This article served a much different purpose: it offered real-world substantial data about how the economy could rebound and gave my clients reason to (quoting the article) "look for opportunity amid adversity."[96] And it worked.

"Oh my goodness," said one client. "I was really shaken, and I was losing confidence. And then I saw this article and realized we, too, can rebound."

Many responded in a similar fashion.

This experience with my clients illustrates something powerful I've learned about the nature of confidence. Confidence is fragile: it can be easily shaken. What was so alarming about the 2020 coronavirus was that, after years of taken-for-granted stability and skyrocketing economic growth, we seemed to suddenly lose confidence in everything: our supply chains, our health (of ourselves and our families), the security of our jobs, the schools in which we entrust our children, the healthcare facilities where we go when sick—confidence that we can go to the store and purchase everyday supplies like toilet paper!

Sometimes a short-term pep talk or an inspiring article can help instill

When leaders, managers, or facilitators help build confidence on their teams, they can inspire others to achieve audacious, improbable goals.

confidence when it's been shaken. After all, we all want to operate from a place of confidence. Confidence is satisfaction, contentment, the sense that your life has forward momentum—the moment you have trust in yourself and the world around you. When you have confidence, even the hard stuff doesn't seem so daunting because you have the bravery and courage to face it. When leaders, managers, or facilitators help build confidence on their teams, they can inspire others to achieve audacious, improbable goals.

Confidence is our final and sixth C. It's the icing on the cake of human need—and we all know that cake tastes lousy without the frosting. Confidence is the culmination or crescendo of human fulfillment that you can attain once everything else is satisfied. The other five facets of human needs (Cs) are a precondition for confidence. After all, if you don't have clarity, you don't have confidence; if you aren't connected to others, you don't have confidence; if you're not contributing, you can't have confidence. When you address all these other needs, you can then turn to confidence and keep the following in mind. Whether it's in ourselves, our teams, our companies, or our markets, confidence requires constant calibration. Our businesses, financial markets, and lives are uncertain, and when extenuating events arise, our human instinct is to simply respond and react. To have true confidence, we must constantly plan and respond with quiet, sober confidence.

***

That's certainly Dan Sullivan's conclusion. And he should know. The founder and CEO of Strategic Coach Inc., Dan has helped instill entrepreneurial confidence in over twenty thousand entrepreneurs the world over, turning them into powerhouses that improve their businesses by factors of ten or even twenty-five. He's certainly inspired me.

When Dan was a young man of twenty-one years, the army drafted him to serve in the war in Vietnam.[97] One of the most harrowing training exercises involved working with live grenades. The task before him and his recruits: to activate a grenade, throw it over a mound of dirt, and not injure themselves or anyone else in the process.[98] If they needed any reminder about the seriousness of the exercise, the sergeant relayed some stories of soldiers past who'd accidentally detonated and dropped their grenades, resulting in death or maiming.[99] Before the exercise began, the sergeant asked the young recruits whether they were scared. Dan was the only man of the fifty assembled who raised his hand.[100] And the sergeant took note, praising Dan before his colleagues: "Sullivan is the only person here I trust because he's actually telling me what's going on. He's actually telling the truth." "Fear is wetting your pants," his sergeant said. "Courage is doing what you're supposed to do with wet pants."[101]

That statement crystallized something powerful for Dan: people either embrace fear and act courageously despite it, or they embark on any number of courage-avoidance behaviors.[102] The latter sometimes include addictive behaviors, like drugs, gambling, or alcohol, and sometimes psychological behaviors like procrastination or other subtle forms of self-sabotage. Either way, whether we're entrepreneurs, team leaders, or soldiers preparing for battle, our posture toward fear is a critical determinant to our success.[103]

And what's the difference between courage and confidence, the final C in my framework? It's simple: courage feels bad, while confidence feels awesome. Confidence is the end goal, and it takes some difficulty getting there. We must first commit to a goal, like going to war or embarking on a new building plan, and then we have to create the capability to pursue and achieve that goal, even in the face of fear, difficulty, and adversity (like a grenade exploding or a pandemic shuttering your business). That's a crucial point. We aren't naturally born with confidence, and we shouldn't expect it—confidence is the end point or the reward for enduring pain, uncertainty, and discomfort. As Dan notes: "The truth is that everyone, in everything they do on a daily basis, is striving for greater confidence. Everyone loves the feeling of confidence: the sense of certainty and serenity that makes everything feel 'right.' In our daydreams and fantasies, we wish we could always feel this way."[104]

DR. TRICIA'S TAKE

Bridging the gap between nature and nurture by understanding the need for **confidence**

Human beings need to feel confident. Understanding the full impact of confidence requires a distinction between three similar concepts: self-efficacy (i.e., the degree to which an individual feels they have the ability to influence the outcomes of their own lives), self-esteem (i.e., the relatively stable sense of worth), and self-confidence (i.e., the strength of one's expectations for performance and self-evaluation of one's own abilities).[105] This distinction is important, as we often assume a team member with high self-esteem is also confident. This is not necessarily the case; an individual can feel generally positive about themselves yet have a lower assessment of their own abilities to accomplish particular goals. In the field of personality psychology, this correlates with traits (i.e., relatively enduring) and states (i.e., situationally influences).[106]

Confidence matters for performance. Individuals who lack confidence cannot perform to their potential. The Theory of Planned Behavior, proposed by Icek Ajzen, demonstrates how beliefs can exercise a profound impact on behavioral outcomes.[107] This theory suggests an individual's beliefs about their own ability and control over an outcome, along with subjective norms, are the precursors for intentions to perform; intention to perform is the antecedent to behavior. In other words, before a team member can achieve a result, they must first expect a positive outcome and believe they have the abilities necessary to succeed. Absent those foundational components of belief, individuals might take on job tasks out of duty or assignment but will struggle to achieve their full potential. This can lead to suboptimal performance and in exchange can result in disappointment or resentment from other team members.

Others impact our confidence. Confidence is not solely dependent upon an individual and can be influenced by many external factors. Self-confidence is influenced by both internal and external sources.[108] The personal recognition of accomplishments (e.g., "I'm so proud of myself for running that marathon!") or the relationship we have with our own inner monologue / self-talk (i.e., are you your own friend or foe?) both influence our sense of self. The feedback, care, and concern we receive from your friends, family, and colleagues can likewise serve as external sources of self-confidence.

These external sources are important for teams. Our own sense of self can be impacted both positively or negatively when we observe those closest to us succeed (especially when we feel our abilities are similar to theirs) and when trusted colleagues provide words of encouragement. When team members we judge to be less skilled succeed, or when similarly skilled team members fail, our own self-confidence can likewise take a hit. Harsh words from a trusted colleague or a lack of sorely needed encouragement can also be detrimental to self-confidence.

The unknown can also undermine our confidence. I will often coach teams that their biggest confidence boost will be in productive feedback practices. I'll often say, "You want someone to tell you if you've got something in your teeth." Glimpsing a mirror hours after lunch and realizing you've spoken with many team members with broccoli in your teeth can be a huge strike to confidence. Teams who practice good feedback techniques have increased individual and group confidence. Be real with people about their strengths and development needs, let them know the reasons for decisions, and provide ongoing peer coaching.

Teams who are aware of their impact on one another and incorporate these strategies build confidence and increase performance.

The much-vaunted story of Apple, especially under founder Steve Jobs, provides a beautiful illustration of the corporate lifecycle of confidence. I hesitate to write anything about Jobs, as he's been the subject of endless speculation and adulation. His biographer Walter Isaacson ascribes him mythical status, saying he belongs among such luminaries as Walt Disney, Thomas Edison, and Henry Ford.[109] Here's what we know for sure: he created a company in 1976, was fired from it nine years later, and returned to rescue it from the brink of bankruptcy in 1997. The next milestone in his life was bittersweet: when he died of cancer in 2011, he had created the most important and the most valuable company the globe had ever seen.[110] But sometimes when we examine his legacy, we tend to get lost in his "genius" instead of focusing on Steve the human. Steve was someone committed to leaning into his fears with courage, as Dan Sullivan suggests all successful entrepreneurs (and human beings) must.

Jobs learned, for example, during his first tenure at his company that micromanaging others with an iron fist didn't bring out their best.

During his second round at Apple, he learned from this managerial misstep and changed course. He famously became confident enough to not only hire people smarter than him but encourage them to exert independence and tell him when he was wrong. "The more mature and confident he became," notes a *Fast Company* profile, "the more he surrounded himself with strong, opinionated executives who felt comfortable arguing with him. This was something he had learned during his exile from Apple."[111] He encouraged the entire team to take ownership of the organization, and because of that confidence he instilled in them, they were able to create the technology behemoth we know today. "Apple's resurrection was a team effort, a fact that gets overlooked to the detriment of everyone," *Fast Company* continues.[112] His company's astonishing success doesn't owe to unique genius and preternatural managerial ability—he created a culture of confidence the old-fashioned way, through learning from his mistakes. Just before he died in 2011, the newly minted CEO of Apple, Tim Cook, circulated the following memo: "I want you to be confident that Apple is not going to change … I am confident our best years lie ahead of us and that together we will continue to make Apple the magical place that it is."[113] A beautiful way to honor and perpetuate Steve's philosophy.

Perhaps an even more inspiring story of the adversity to confidence arc is Sara Blakely, the founder and CEO of Spanx. Unlike most of us, Blakely didn't have to grudgingly admit that failure led to wisdom. Her father drilled that into her and her sibling from a young age. During her childhood dinners, Dad routinely asked them the following: "What have you failed at this week?"[114] "My dad growing up encouraged me and my brother to fail. The gift he was giving me is that failure is (when you are) not trying versus the outcome. It's really allowed me to be much freer in trying things and spreading my wings in life."[115]

And fail she did. As a child, she conceived of the idea of "charm socks," sewing plastic pieces onto socks and hawking them at school (not to sound harsh, but that never took off, so I'm labeling it a failure).[116] She failed at becoming a lawyer, not managing to pass the law school entrance examination twice. She then went to Disney World auditioning to be Goofy—that one ended in failure, too, because she was too short to pull it off.[117] She was a total failure as a traveling fax machine salesperson (in a failing industry to boot!), as she was so nervous to approach potential clients that she often broke down in tears and procrastinated by driving around.[118] Then, one magical day in 1998, she looked at herself in the mirror and, feeling dissatisfied with her posterior, conceived of the idea of Spanx.[119] You have to admit, the idea was great and resonates strongly with most females. But it was hardly novel—people had been wearing girdles, pantyhose, and Lululemon pants for ages, all with the aim of flattering their figures. It would have been easy for her to quit—after all, she'd failed so many times.

Instead of shriveling at the prospect of more failure, she committed to her vision. Women needed this product, she insisted, and she persevered for two years of more rejection.[120] "It didn't faze me," she recalls, "I didn't have a special ability, it was sheer drive and telling myself to keep going."[121] She continued to lean into her business ignorance, reframing her lack of knowledge in business, retail, and clothing design as an asset: "What you don't know can become your greatest asset if you'll let it and if you have the confidence to say, I'm going to do it anyway even though I haven't been taught or somebody hasn't shown me the way," she said.[122] Notice there that Blakely confirms Dan Sullivan's connection between discomfort and confidence—this time substituting fear for ignorance. Her ignorance can even be funny and charming, like when she did an interview with the BBC and extolled her product's ability to smooth and flatten a person's fanny (pro tip: fanny means vagina in Britain!).[123] No matter—she'll just keep learning and celebrating her success. "Blakely's embrace of failure," notes a CNBC profile, "has helped make her the youngest self-made female billionaire in America."[124]

It's Blakely's unique form of confidence that makes her story so powerful and inspirational. Often in the Business Lab, when I'm coaching executive teams, people look to me for a nod of approval and by extension for the confidence they need. I understand the human vulnerability at stake—when we're faced with touch decisions, we oftentimes seek validation from others. We look outside of ourselves. But when people look to me for this validation, and even worse—when they have more confidence in me than in themselves—I immediately change course. "Stop looking at me," I'll say. "Look to yourself."

And guess what? Sometimes we'll have the best data; we'll step forth in confidence and make a major organizational challenge. And we'll still fail. Oftentimes I encounter this in the lab as well—executives whose confidence is damaged because of a failure. And that's normal. And I normalize this for my clients, ensuring them that this is typical. But how do you catapult from a failure to a position of renewed confidence? That's where having a growth mindset is so powerful. That involves taking and receiving feedback in vulnerability and moving forward.

One of my clients, with about twenty employees, operates from a faith-based perspective. Everyone there believes that they can positively influence their clients by operating from a place of goodness, having integrity, and being of service. Whenever faced with a failure, they say, "Thank you, God, for this opportunity to grow." Whether you subscribe to the underlying belief system or not, this is a powerful growth mindset—by repeating it like a mantra, it helps bake a growth mindset into the very fabric of their company. Their confidence derives from belief, and this gives them the resiliency to endure the highs and lows, the successes and failures, of business.

Most recently, this company's leadership team has had to transition from the original founder to someone new. They're all figuring out how to allow someone else to take charge of the team and maintain confidence in them, when they all instinctually want to defer to the original founder. In challenging new people to assume the mantle of leadership, they are also reflecting on how the culture needs to shift as well. The new person is capable but lacks the consideration, caring, and empathy of the older leader. After thanking God for this new challenge, we convened in the Business Lab and mapped out a one-year plan to migrate this person into leadership, all the while reflecting on any larger cultural changes necessary at the organization. We're all confident that they'll get through this.

To maintain personal confidence, we must constantly work on ourselves. And one of the most powerful ways of doing that is journaling. It's such a quick and powerful way to gain confidence. Some people have gratitude and appreciation journals, where they record three things for which they are grateful each day. The more grateful and appreciative we are, the happier and more joyful we'll become. Your brain will secrete endorphins, and you'll start to feel great about yourself—confident in your abilities to face the future. This has positive multiplier effects as joyful, appreciative people radiate confidence and inspire it in others. This will in turn inspire trust in you.

While this is an individual and solitary activity, we can generalize the practice to our teams as well. Just like regularly checking in with ourselves, we can do the same in our groups, asking teams, "What did you fail at last week, month, or quarter?" "How did you succeed?" Whether you do it on a weekly, monthly, or quarterly basis, check in with everyone, reminding them of their excellence in certain projects, their capacity to overcome hardship, and where growth areas lie. Ask what Sara Blakely's father did: "How did you fail today?" Once your colleagues acknowledge the failure, give them some encouragement and ask them what they learned and how they'd act differently in the future. Make failure and learning from failure something to embrace. Team members shrouded in fear, apprehension, and doubt run from failure. If people feel that failure could make them lose their jobs, they're back to Maslow's lowest rung of need, trying to maintain basic security. But admitting failure and learning from it helps create a growth mindset—it opens space for trust and courage in teams and organizations, as people know they can learn and improve in a climate of trust.

Most mistakes we make in business aren't major, even though managers and leaders treat them as such. I'm not of course speaking about leadership teams, where mistakes can result in major problems. But that actually makes the imperative to embrace risk even higher, as managers must be able to share failures and learn from them. Not only will this lend clarity to the team's mission, but it will help inspire confidence in the team so that you can face any challenge—including a global pandemic.

***

Even as the coronavirus was enveloping the world, I was experiencing a different crisis of confidence when writing this book. It started when I began the clarity chapter. When you have a new idea, just like in business when you create a new service or pioneer a new product, you begin to see evidence of it everywhere. Same thing happens when you buy a car: you never gave the Lexus hybrid RX any thought until you bought one, and now you see a lot of them on the freeways. That's the reticular activator in the brain clicking in, showing evidence of everything.

And then I was driving home from Indianapolis, listening to TED talks on the topic of how there's nothing new under the sun. There's nothing new in the world, the talks seemed to suggest—there's an assembly of preexisting thought that's more or less set, and all that's new is our perspective on it. And my confidence drained more.

"Everyone's talking about human needs," I said to myself.

But then I thought a little more and realized, yes, that's true. Everyone was doing one-offs of clarity, confidence, and consideration. But no one had yet integrated all of these into a holistic picture of how they all might converge, on our teams and in our organizations, to help improve the human experience and helps us achieve new organizational and performance heights. So I took a deep breath, reviewed my 6 Facets of Human Needs (6 Cs), leaned into a position of confidence, and wrote this book.

As **Ashley Baker** likes to joke, "No one goes into HR on purpose." Take this as some insider's humor for human resources (HR) specialists like Ashley. True to the saying, Ashley stumbled into the profession by accident. She was always an idealist and went to school to pursue her passion for adolescent studies and youth ministry. She loved Jesus and kids. Unfortunately, something happened to Ashley in college, and she couldn't continue. She lost confidence.

A little unmoored from the experience, she started working as a temp at a food manufacturer, filling in for an HR manager away on maternity leave. She was only supposed to work for six weeks. But six weeks turned into six months—and HR gradually became Ashley's passion. In 2007, the company hired her permanently. She started as an HR assistant and was later promoted to HR administrator and HR generalist. These promotions were exciting, and she transferred to a different food manufacturer, thinking she wanted to climb the corporate ladder.

Here's the problem: each rung she scaled on that ladder, the further she migrated from her passion. And the less confident she became. "I realized that I had stopped remembering people's names and started remembering their employee ID numbers instead," she recalls. She loved HR because it was related to her primary passion for ministry and love of people. If there was one thing she was confident about, it was her ability to help others. "When no one else could find the answer, I knew who to call or how to get it." She enthusiastically soaked up different laws about workers' compensation and other workplace policies so she could be most helpful.

People gravitated to Ashley and her confidence. Her coworkers would often remark, "You are the only person who can fire someone and they leave smiling." They might have lost their job, but they'd gained their freedom. If something wasn't working, Ashley was able to speak to that part and help energize people about the future possibilities that awaited them. Don't get me wrong—Ashley is extremely kind and never wanted to deliver tough news. But whether the news was good or bad, she woke up every day confident that she could address human needs as an HR specialist, navigate the gray areas, and reframe negative news as powerful possibilities.

Unfortunately, her role shifted from ministering to people to extinguishing fires. Instead of proactively helping people, she was increasingly called upon to address crisis after crisis. Someone on the third shift cut off his finger; another one fell asleep and damaged equipment. Her phone rang night and day with problems like these, all requiring immediate resolution. Someone, for example, might be late for work and managers asked for her to level a consequence. But Ashley pressed: Why was the person late? "That mattered," she recalls, "because at my core, I'm a people person. And to address people's need, I need more information about them." Removed from the people, Ashley's confidence suffered. And so did her happiness. She didn't want to climb anymore.

Since 2017, Ashley has worked for a small family-owned company. Instead of major conglomerates in the Fortune 500 and 100 categories, where she'd worked prior, this mom-and-pop operation in the industrial distribution field employs 150 people in total and is now in its third generation of family leadership. "I never knew confidence was a need at work until I started here," she says. On occasion, the company meets, for example, to discuss individual employees. "Well, Joe called and said he hurt his back again," someone might say. And Ashley's expression plummets because it's too personal— discussing a person's medical issues is also borderline unethical. If before she was only interacting with employee numbers and not enough with actual people, now she's interacting with people a little too intimately!

Ashley and her company face enormous challenges. When we last spoke, they were enduring the worst of the COVID-19 epidemic and trying to assure employees. The average tenure within the company, moreover, is twenty-two years, and in the next three to five years, she plans to lose hundreds of years of accumulated experience at the company. "We're really focusing on building that bench and ensuring we don't lose any of that tribal knowledge that everyone has gleaned over decades," says Ashley, all the while calibrating it to a new generation of workers with a distinct set of workplace needs. Developing a workforce to meet new needs for the company will be a challenge. But knowing she can work with individuals makes Ashley confident in her ability to address these challenges and help steer the company to a productive future. "I'm so excited about it," she says, reflecting on future possibilities, "I really love employee development, and I can't wait to devise accountability charts and hit developmental needs and milestones." This family-owned operation has survived seventy-two years, and Ashley is confident its best seventy-two are yet to come.

Six questions to ask about confidence:

1. How well do you as a leader, manager, or facilitator embrace failure?

2. What are you doing to encourage a growth mindset on the team?

3. Do you do the tough stuff? Does the team get real, open, and honest?

4. Do all team members have, and take, time to work on the business?

5. Do you journal or keep a gratitude list?

6. Are you developing new skills and capabilities in yourself and/or the team?

CONFIDENCE · CLARITY · CONSIDERATION · CONNECTION · CHALLENGE · CONTRIBUTION

SIX
FACETS
of
HUMAN
NEEDS

CONCLUSION

Nature Needs Nurture

S ue Jones (a pseudonym for privacy), who serves on a leadership team overseeing talent development and management, was an enigma to her colleagues and me. On the one hand, she possessed excellent skill and capacity in working with people, which added considerable value to her organization. On the other hand, she lacked courage and confidence and frustrated her team with time-wasting excessive requests for reassurance and periodic lack of follow-through. Over the years, she'd developed a fixed mindset around certain difficult topics, where she resisted feedback, declined challenging assignments, and lapsed into complacency.

When I began coaching Sue's leadership team, I picked up on her behavior and its positive and negative consequences. During one of my Business Laboratory off-site sessions with the eight-person leadership team, we all considered how the leaders could serve and support the organization's employees so they could perform at their best. A significant portion of the team felt that Sue was underperforming in this area and whining a lot in the process. She continually asked for reassurance and for a constant analysis of every interaction with employees: "Did I say this right?" "Am I doing all right?" etc.

Unfortunately, the frustrations being discussed escalated into displays of anger at Sue, so I called for a break. She left the room, breaking down and crying in the restroom. "I think I might need to just quit," she said to me between sobs. "They don't really want me here." "That's not what I'm seeing," I responded. "I see a team that is frustrated but cares about you and wants to fix this." Also, I reflected that there seemed to be more behind her reactions than just what was going on in the organization or at this meeting.

Even in Sue's compromised state, I didn't sugarcoat the situation or offer false reassurance. For her to stay in the company, I insisted, she needed to change. But I also reminded her that although the team was frustrated, they seemed to care for her and that everyone simply wanted to trust her. She needed to return to the team, acknowledge their reservations, and make herself worthy of their trust by changing course. We returned to the meeting where Sue expressed a sheepish resolve to change. Before continuing the meeting, I reminded the group that "this is about principles above personalities," urging them to stick with the facts and to refrain from displaying too much emotion or leveling personal attacks. "Our goal is to build trust and come up with solutions as a team."

The team, genuinely wanting a solution, listened with openness as Sue shared that some of her behaviors and reactions were the result of a past traumatic experience and that she wanted to overcome that obstacle to be a better leader and producer in the organization. With

160

a better understanding of her situation and challenges, the leadership team proposed actions to "right the ship." They established a coaching program for feedback and confidence, and systems and processes for her to better manage her job. Sue felt *considered*, and the team had *clarity*. They then outlined expectations for future *contributions* and *challenges* so that the appropriate outcomes could be achieved for the team and the organization. They had *connected* on a new level and were ready to move forward with an increased level of trust. There was, however, still a gap between Sue's *need* for *confidence* and her lack of confidence.

In addition to the coaching she would be receiving, I recommended Sue read a specific book about confidence that could help her begin to reframe the entire encounter. After reading the book, she began to reconsider the leadership discussion not as an aggressive takedown but as a caring exercise in feedback. And even more crucially, she decided to accept the feedback and do something about it. This was the beginning of an educational journey, including more reading, videos, and online courses. Armed with new knowledge, she began understanding her constant need for approval as a gap in social acceptance and began to understand the true reasons why she felt so needy and constantly whined to her colleagues. Much of her challenge was rooted in a devastating assault she had experienced and the counterproductive defense mechanisms she'd enacted since then. What a breakthrough! Gradually her need for constant reassurance lessened as she felt confident that she belonged in her company and that her colleagues trusted and cared for her.

In addition to becoming more effective in her position, Sue joined a corporate board at a leading industry organization, where she helps educate and mentor people in her profession at a director level. She exercises influence on the executive decision-making at her company and has pioneered several programs helping the entire organization adopt a growth mindset culture. Leading by example, she models the type of behavior she seeks in the organization, such as proactively receiving feedback from her boss and her peers, mentoring direct reports in human needs, and constantly learning.

Sue made such an impression on me because her story spans the entire nature-to-nurture developmental spectrum. She began her journey as we all do, as a complex human being with certain difficulties and pain points arising from personal obstacles. Even so, she managed to accomplish what I call a "failure turnaround." The failure turnaround refers to looking at our failures with honesty and courage, accepting these failures as learning experiences with gratitude, deriving lessons from them, and moving forward. Sue mustered the courage to accept peer criticism and endure a little pain, realizing in the process she needed to change. Sue's journey for change encompasses the 6 Cs outlined in this book: *clarity* of her role, *connection* to the team, *contribution* to the organization, *challenge* to be a better leader, *consideration* as a human being, and the *confidence* to take effective action. Because these needs have been met, the way in which she receives nurturing at her company can be more effective.

Human nature is vital and important, and *nature needs nurture*. There's a dynamism between nature and nurture that's akin to fertilizing our crops. To grow, plants have needs—their six 6 Cs involve having a rich and nutritious soil base in which they can implant a sturdy root structure, enabling them to grow to maturity and produce rich harvests. Absent nutrient-rich soil, plants don't receive their vital needs and remain undernourished. If we attend to the basic nutrition of our crops, we can create the conditions for a sturdy root base and from this foundation nurture our plants to produce consistent and delicious fruit over many seasons. This process sometimes involves returning to the soil, identifying a nutritional need that's lacking, and reapplying it. The same is true with people—if we address their vital needs, we create a sturdy foundation from which we can nurture them to performance and achievement heights.

Sue was like many people in our workforce today, desperately in need of a coach or mentor to enable such growth. I was disheartened, though not surprised, to read a 2019 study about the lack of mentorship and coaching relationships in our workforce.[125] Over three-quarters of Americans, the study found, actively wanted a mentor, but a mere 37 percent actually had one. And most of those 37 percent felt shortchanged in these mentorship arrangements because they were too focused on professional concerns, and not enough on caring for them as human beings. This comes as no surprise to those of us who are professional coaches and facilitators. I wrote this book to address this lack of leadership, coaching, and mentorship support in the workplace and to introduce you to my discovered framework: the 6 Facets of Human Needs. With the application of the 6 Cs, people can become more satisfied and effective at work, and managers can achieve longer-lasting results from employee engagement, soft-skills trainings, team-building activities, and coaching/mentoring programs.

The people on our teams have "human moments," and we need to embrace the fact that "human happens" in our organizations in order to enact real change and nurture stronger outcomes.

As we've seen throughout this book in general, and in the case of Sue Jones in particular, if we can't overcome our self-preservation and social acceptance instincts, we can't succeed on our teams and in our companies. The people on our teams have "human moments," and we need to embrace the fact that "human happens" in our organizations in order to enact real change and nurture stronger outcomes. If we're dwelling only in the realm of human instinct, with our six human needs constantly going unmet, we become vulnerable to disengagement and burnout—a sad social epidemic devastating our workplaces.

Burnout has become such a widespread phenomenon that in May of 2019, the World Health Organization recognized it not as a medical problem that we can overcome with yoga classes, warm baths, and therapy but as an occupational problem that is exacting an enormous human and financial toll.[126] Consider these breathtaking statistics: burnout costs the global economy $1 trillion annually, it's responsible for $190 billion in healthcare costs and 120,000 deaths in the United States alone, and in stressful industries and companies, healthcare costs are 50 percent greater than nonstressful ones.[127] Stressed or burned-out employees can't focus on succeeding in their roles and contributing to their teams. They instead spend their days away from the job sick, zapping life from their colleagues and teams, or scanning job boards for opportunities with better work environments.

* * *

As a manager, leader, or facilitator, addressing human nature, meeting the needs of your people, and nurturing others begins with you. Remember the airplane rule? In the unlikely event of decreasing cabin pressure aboard an aircraft, all passengers ensure their oxygen masks are firmly fixed before helping others. Sue Jones couldn't effectively coach others—her defining professional strength—until she had fixed the human-needs gap within herself. Please make sure you've done the personal work and addressed your own needs before helping others. Seek a mentor, coach, or professional EOS implementer like me for help with enhancing your management capabilities, learning to lead by example, and getting more out of your people and teams.

When you help yourself and then turn your talents to helping others, you'll join me in seeing how wonderful, fascinating, and rich people truly are. Yes, people are complicated and flawed, but just like our crops, they are capable of extraordinary growth and bountiful harvests. In our organizations, people are our best assets. Top leaders at companies consistently state that people make all the difference in team and organizational success. Your success hinges on your ability to influence and harness this vital human energy. When we address the 6 Facets of Human Needs (6 Cs) and nurture our people, there's no end to what we can achieve as individuals, teams, and organizations as a whole.

I challenge you to join me in discovering new facets to human beings and to tune into to the remarkable ways in which people can grow. They might surprise you. As you focus on needs and improve the workplace environment, you'll increase the effectiveness of your people and teams, and they, and you, will end up less frustrated and more satisfied. You've signed up for a beautiful journey with humanity at work—the journey to create a stronger and healthier Human Team!

AWARENESS-ACCEPTANCE-ACTION

Awareness. Become fascinated by the people on your team(s) by learning more about human nature and needs because "human moments" will happen.

Acceptance. Accept yourself and be vulnerable—as you practice what you've learned, you will become a more confident leader. Accept that people on your team are whole human beings and that "human happens" (meaning they will act like humans!). And be sure to get your team members accepting feedback (considering the way they like or need to receive it).

Action. Explore the Team Health Assessment in this book. Download and use the free coaching guide designed to help you nurture your people to stronger outcomes (**www.Business-Alchemist.com/TheHumanTeam**). And finally, keep this book as a guide on your journey so that you can refer back to the chapters that cover the 6 Cs. With this knowledge and the support from your coach and team, you'll be a more effective manager. Remember, confidence comes from doing. Get started now. Your people *need* your coaching, mentoring, and leadership!

6 FACETS OF
HUMAN NEEDS™

Team Health Assessment

As a leader/manager, use this assessment to determine if the 6 Facets of Human Needs are being met on your team. This will help you determine the health of your team and areas that need nurturing in order to arrive at engagement, effectiveness, and successful outcomes. Scoring accuracy increases the more people on the team who provide feedback on this assessment. You can also use this as an individual coaching and mentoring tool by simply converting the questions to be relevant for an individual team member.

CLARITY

Our team has a clearly articulated strategy/plan.

☐ **1** Strongly Disagree ☐ **2** Disagree ☐ **3** Neutral ☐ **4** Agree ☐ **5** Strongly Agree

Each member of our team takes ownership of and is responsible for the strategy and/or plan.

☐ **1** Strongly Disagree ☐ **2** Disagree ☐ **3** Neutral ☐ **4** Agree ☐ **5** Strongly Agree

All processes and procedures needed to execute the strategic plan are documented and clear for all involved.

☐ **1** Strongly Disagree ☐ **2** Disagree ☐ **3** Neutral ☐ **4** Agree ☐ **5** Strongly Agree

CONNECTION

Our team participates in regular team-building and trust-building exercises and activities.

☐ **1** Strongly Disagree ☐ **2** Disagree ☐ **3** Neutral ☐ **4** Agree ☐ **5** Strongly Agree

Our team engages in meaningful meetings (e.g., huddles, standing meetings, formal meetings) on a regular basis.

☐ **1** Strongly Disagree ☐ **2** Disagree ☐ **3** Neutral ☐ **4** Agree ☐ **5** Strongly Agree

All team members, whether local or virtual, are provided formats for effective engagement.

☐ **1** Strongly Disagree ☐ **2** Disagree ☐ **3** Neutral ☐ **4** Agree ☐ **5** Strongly Agree

CONTRIBUTION

It is evident each team member is contributing their best version of themselves to the team.

☐ **1** Strongly Disagree ☐ **2** Disagree ☐ **3** Neutral ☐ **4** Agree ☐ **5** Strongly Agree

Team members regularly engage in developing skills/knowledge that are/is shared with the team.

☐ **1** Strongly Disagree ☐ **2** Disagree ☐ **3** Neutral ☐ **4** Agree ☐ **5** Strongly Agree

Team members feel their work is meaningful.

☐ **1** Strongly Disagree ☐ **2** Disagree ☐ **3** Neutral ☐ **4** Agree ☐ **5** Strongly Agree

CHALLENGE

Team members all have high levels of trust (with the team as a whole and with individuals on the team).

☐ **1** Strongly Disagree ☐ **2** Disagree ☐ **3** Neutral ☐ **4** Agree ☐ **5** Strongly Agree

Team members utilize development opportunities (e.g., coaching, training, 360 surveys, feedback loops).

☐ **1** Strongly Disagree ☐ **2** Disagree ☐ **3** Neutral ☐ **4** Agree ☐ **5** Strongly Agree

Team members respectfully handle conflict in a proactive way.

☐ **1** Strongly Disagree ☐ **2** Disagree ☐ **3** Neutral ☐ **4** Agree ☐ **5** Strongly Agree

CONSIDERATION

Team recognition processes (e.g., rewards) are meaningful and tied to team values and beneficial outcomes.

☐ **1** Strongly Disagree   ☐ **2** Disagree   ☐ **3** Neutral   ☐ **4** Agree   ☐ **5** Strongly Agree

Team members have regular 1:1s that are not scheduled over / disregarded as a low priority.

☐ **1** Strongly Disagree   ☐ **2** Disagree   ☐ **3** Neutral   ☐ **4** Agree   ☐ **5** Strongly Agree

Team members have shared their preferences for recognition and feedback / the team leader knows how each team member prefers to be recognized.

☐ **1** Strongly Disagree   ☐ **2** Disagree   ☐ **3** Neutral   ☐ **4** Agree   ☐ **5** Strongly Agree

CONFIDENCE

Team leader embraces failure as a growth and learning opportunity.

☐ **1** Strongly Disagree   ☐ **2** Disagree   ☐ **3** Neutral   ☐ **4** Agree   ☐ **5** Strongly Agree

Team engages in candid conversations to uncover sources of failure and opportunities for improvement.

☐ **1** Strongly Disagree   ☐ **2** Disagree   ☐ **3** Neutral   ☐ **4** Agree   ☐ **5** Strongly Agree

All team members take time to work "on" the business, not just "in" the business.

☐ **1** Strongly Disagree   ☐ **2** Disagree   ☐ **3** Neutral   ☐ **4** Agree   ☐ **5** Strongly Agree

GENERAL

Our team is capable of committing to the changes necessary to enhance or maintain the team dynamics.

☐ **1** Strongly Disagree   ☐ **2** Disagree   ☐ **3** Neutral   ☐ **4** Agree   ☐ **5** Strongly Agree

Our team is willing to actively manage weaknesses in our team functioning in a healthy, cohesive way.

☐ **1** Strongly Disagree   ☐ **2** Disagree   ☐ **3** Neutral   ☐ **4** Agree   ☐ **5** Strongly Agree

TOTAL SCORE _____

Scoring:

90–100: Very strong! Ensure you have institutionalized these team traits/actions.

61–89: Some effective or marginally effective team functioning. Pinpoint which facets are the teams' opportunities, but don't forget to pinpoint the facets that are strengths—and keep feeding those positive actions.

41–60: Some areas are approaching positive trends.

20–40: Low functioning; team toxicity risk.

Note: Low scores in any one of these areas indicate a need to dig in to developing that facet of human need (Clarity, Connection, Contribution, Challenge, Consideration, or Confidence) in an individual, the team, or the organization. Keep in mind that the 6 Facets of Human Needs are interconnected. You might have an issue just under the surface in another area or have a blind spot regarding team or individual functioning if only one area is rated low.

ABOUT THE AUTHOR

Jeanet Wade's focus is always on building healthy teams and healthy bottom lines. As the first Certified EOS Implementer™ in the St. Louis region, facilitating, teaching, and coaching the Entrepreneurial Operating System® (EOS®) to leadership teams at privately held companies, she developed a reputation for helping clients get Traction® on their Vision by leveraging her experience in marketing, innovation, and management. Because of her passion for people and insights into the basic human needs that must be met in order to fully actualize the potential of a team, she quickly became known as the go-to resource for how to have effective, healthy teams that allow businesses to harness their people energy and maximize their "Return on Individual." Jeanet was also named one of 100 St. Louisans You Should Know to Succeed in Business by *St. Louis Small Business Monthly*.

For more about Jeanet, visit her website,
www.Business-Alchemist.com, or follow her on LinkedIn,
www.linkedin.com/in/jeanet-wade-ab5500.

OUR SERVICES

For more on our service offering and to engage Jeanet Wade for speaking engagements, visit **www.Business-Alchemist.com**.

At the Business Alchemist website you can watch videos, read blogs, listen to interviews, and download the complimentary coaching guide for *The Human Team*.

ENDNOTES

1   "Understanding the Stress Response," *Harvard Health Publishing*, updated May 1, 2018, https://www.health.harvard.edu/staying-healthy/understanding-the-stress-response.

2   Joseph Ledoux, "'Run, Hide, Fight' Is Not How Our Brains Work," *New York Times*, December 18, 2015, https://www.nytimes.com/2015/12/20/opinion/sunday/run-hide-fight-is-not-how-our-brains-work.html.

3   Ledoux, "'Run, Hide, Fight.'"

4   Ledoux, "'Run, Hide, Fight.'"

5   Ledoux, "'Run, Hide, Fight.'"

6   Ledoux, "'Run, Hide, Fight.'"

7   Sandra E. Garcia, "Jazmine Barnes Case Shows How Trauma Can Affect Memory," *New York Times*, January 6, 2019, https://www.nytimes.com/2019/01/06/science/stress-trauma-eyewitness-events.html.

8   Adam Liptak, "34 Years Later, Supreme Court Will Revisit Eyewitness IDs," *New York Times*, August 22, 2011, https://www.nytimes.com/2011/08/23/us/23bar.html?scp=1&sq=liptAK%20EYEWTINESS%20PERRY&st=cse.

9   Please note, this is journalist Adam Liptak's paraphrase of Professor Garrett's book: Liptak, "34 Years Later."

10   Liptak, "34 Years Later."

11 "Creating Psychological Safety in the Workplace," *Harvard Business Review*, January 22, 2019, https://hbr.org/podcast/2019/01/creating-psychological-safety-in-the-workplace.

12 "Creating Psychological Safety in the Workplace."

13 "Advanced Client Systems," *Stevechandler.com*, accessed February 9, 2020, https://www.stevechandler.com/Advanced_Client_Systems_program.html.

14 Penny Singer, "An Unusual Tool in Hiring the Right Person," *New York Times*, September 27, 1998, https://www.nytimes.com/1998/09/27/nyregion/an-unusual-tool-in-hiring-the-right-person.html.

15 Singer, "An Unusual Tool."

16 Singer, "An Unusual Tool" (italics mine).

17 "Understanding the Conversation Gap: Why Employees Aren't Talking, and What We Can Do about It," *Bravely*, accessed February 22, 2020, https://learn.workbravely.com/hubfs/Understanding-the-Conversation-Gap.pdf?t=1533596048056&utm_campaign=smart%20brief%20test&utm_source=hs_automation&utm_medium=email&utm_content=64321921&_hsenc=p2ANqtz-_4k_KzRnQlCrerxB5Gr0XEMMWshlLmigMT3ElhTx6htsOUK-3kcp7H-J_GAqZMvIAdILhbkkDX2sEDVSXIQdx9e-xqh8A&_hsmi=64321921.

18 *Merriam-Webster*, s.v., "clarity," accessed April 2, 2020, https://www.merriam-webster.com/dictionary/clarity?src=search-dict-hed.

19 "APA Dictionary of Psychology," *American Psychological Association*, accessed April 2, 2020, https://dictionary.apa.org/confusion.

20 Trey Hedden and John Gabrieli, "The Ebb and Flow of Attention in the Human Brain," *Nature Neuroscience* 9, no. 7 (2006): 863–65, https://doi.org/10.1038/nn0706-863.

21   Michael Schneider, "Most People Handle Difficult Situations by Ignoring Them—and the Fallout Isn't Pretty," *Inc*, accessed February 22, 2020, https://www.inc.com/michael-schneider/70-percent-of-employees-avoid-difficult-conversations-their-companies-are-suffering-as-a-result.html.

22   "Understanding the Conversation Gap."

23   Emily Flitter, "The Price of Wells Fargo's Fake Account Scandal Grows by $3 Billion," *New York Times*, February 21, 2020, https://www.nytimes.com/2020/02/21/business/wells-fargo-settlement.html.

24   Flitter, "The Price of Wells Fargo's Fake Account Scandal."

25   Flitter, "The Price of Wells Fargo's Fake Account Scandal."

26   Emily Flitter and Stacy Cowley, "Wells Fargo Says Its Culture Has Changed. Some Employees Disagree," *New York Times*, March 9, 2019, https://www.nytimes.com/2019/03/09/business/wells-fargo-sales-culture.html.

27   Flitter and Cowley, "Wells Fargo Says."

28   Flitter and Cowley, "Wells Fargo Says."

29   Mishka Lysack, "The Teach-In on Global Warming Solutions and Vygotsky: Fostering Ecological Action and Environmental Citizenship," *Journal of Education* 44 (2009): 119–34, https://doi.org/10.1107/s2053229618015838/jx3023sup1.cif.

30   "Scientific Research," *NeuroLeadership Institute*, accessed April 2, 2020, https://neuroleadership.com/research/approach/scientific-research.

31   J. P. Mitchell, C. N. Macrae, and M. R. Banaji, "Dissociable Medial Prefrontal Contributions to Judgments of Similar and Dissimilar Others," *Neuron* 50 (2006): 655–63.

32 T. Singer et al., "Empathic neural responses are modulated by the perceived fairness of others," *Nature* 439 (2006): 466–69.

33 G. Domes et al., "Oxytocin Attenuates Amygdala Responses to Emotional Faces Regardless of Valence," *Biological Psychiatry* 62, no. 10 (2007): 1187–90.

34 Jennifer Robinson, "Workplace Socializing Is Productive: An MIT Researcher Talks about the Usefulness of Water Cooler Chatter," *Gallup Business Journal*, November 13, 2008, http://www.gallup.com/ consulting/52/Employee-Engagement.aspx.

35 Michael Price, "Human Herding: How People Are Like Guppies," *Psychology Today*, June 25, 2013, https://www.psychologytoday.com/us/blog/ darwin-eternity/201306/human-herding-how-people-are-guppies.

36 "David Rock's SCARF Model: Using Neuroscience to Work Effectively With Others," *Mindtools*, accessed April 2, 2020. https://www. mindtools.com/pages/article/SCARF.htm.

37 Brian Resnick, "Have Smartphones Really Destroyed a Generation? We Don't Know," *Vox*, updated May 16, 2019, https:// www.vox.com/science-and-health/2019/2/20/18210498/ smartphones-tech-social-media-teens-depression-anxiety-research.

38 Though please see Resnick's important "Have Smartphones Really Destroyed a Generation?" for important qualifications to this argument.

39 Michael Bible, "Is the US facing an epidemic of 'deaths of despair'? These researchers say yes," *Guardian*, March 28, 2017, https://www.theguardian.com/us-news/2017/mar/28/ deaths-of-despair-us-jobs-drugs-alcohol-suicide.

40 Mark Tarallo, "How to Reduce Employee Turnover through Robust Retention Strategies," *SHRM*, September 17, 2018, https://www. shrm.org/resourcesandtools/hr-topics/talent-acquisition/pages/how-to-reduce-employee-turnover-through-robust-retention-strategies.aspx.

41   Naz Beheshti, "10 Timely Statistics about the Connection Between Employee Engagement and Wellness," *Forbes*, January 16, 2019, https://www.forbes.com/sites/nazbeheshti/2019/01/16/10-timely-statistics-about-the-connection-between-employee-engagement-and-wellness/#54e2823f22a0.

42   Mona Sabet, "This Is the Precise Number of People to Put on a Team to Maximize Productivity," *Fast Company*, November 14, 2019, https://www.fastcompany.com/90429950/this-is-the-precise-number-of-people-to-put-on-a-team-to-maximize-productivity.

43   Sabet, "This Is the Precise Number of People."

44   Christine Ro, "Dunbar's Number: Why We Can Only Maintain 150 Relationships," *BBC*, October 9, 2019, https://www.bbc.com/future/article/20191001-dunbars-number-why-we-can-only-maintain-150-relationships.

45   Ro, "Dunbar's Number."

46   Sabet, "This Is the Precise Number of People."

47   Sabet, "This Is the Precise Number of People."

48   Jacob Morgan, "Why Smaller Teams Are Better than Larger Ones," *Forbes*, April 15, 2015, https://www.forbes.com/sites/jacobmorgan/2015/04/15/why-smaller-teams-are-better-than-larger-ones/#79eaefb11e68.

49   Morgan, "Why Smaller Teams Are Better."

50   "The Work Humans Are Wired to Do," *Psychology Today*, May 23, 2017, https://www.psychologytoday.com/us/blog/the-gen-y-guide/201705/the-work-humans-are-wired-do.

51 Relly Nadler, "Where Did My IQ Go No. 2? Handling the Hijack," *Psychology Today*, May 30, 2011, https://www.psychologytoday.com/us/blog/leading-emotional-intelligence/201105/where-did-my-iq-go-no-2-handling-the-hijack.

52 Andrew E. Budson, "Don't Listen to Your Lizard Brain," *Psychology Today*, December 3, 2017, https://www.psychologytoday.com/us/blog/managing-your-memory/201712/don-t-listen-your-lizard-brain.

53 Renee Jain, "Stop the Amygdala Hijack in Its Tracks!" *GoZen!*, November 15, 2018, https://gozen.com/stop-the-amygdala-hijack-in-its-tracks/.

54 Relly Nadler, "Where Did My IQ Go No. 2? Handling the Hijack," *Psychology Today*, May 30, 2011, https://www.psychologytoday.com/us/blog/leading-emotional-intelligence/201105/where-did-my-iq-go-no-2-handling-the-hijack.

55 Merily Leis, "7 Stories That Prove the Importance of Teamwork," *Scoro*, accessed March 17, 2020, https://www.scoro.com/blog/teamwork-stories-importance-of-teamwork/.

56 Logan Chierotti, "Harvard Professor Says 95% of Purchasing Decisions Are Subconscious," *INC*, March 26, 2018, https://www.inc.com/logan-chierotti/harvard-professor-says-95-of-purchasing-decisions-are-subconscious.html.

57 Specifically, "Most euroscientists would agree that well over 90% of our behavior is generated outside of consciousness": Victor W. Hwang, "What's Better for Business: Logic or Emotion? Answers from Neuroscience," *Forbes*, March 27, 2013, https://www.forbes.com/sites/victorhwang/2013/03/27/whats-better-for-business-logic-or-feelings-answers-from-neuroscience/#38754af8199b.

58 Hwang, "What's Better for Business."

59 "The New ROI: Return on Individuals," *Harvard Business School* (Working Knowledge), September 1, 2003, https://hbswk.hbs.edu/archive/the-new-roi-return-on-individuals.

60 Annamarie Mann and Nate Dvorak, "Employee Recognition: Low Cost, High Impact," *Gallup*, June 28, 2016, https://www.gallup.com/workplace/236441/employee-recognition-low-cost-high-impact.aspx.

61 Martine Haas and Mark Mortensen, "The Secrets of Great Teamwork," *Harvard Business Review*, June 2016, https://hbr.org/2016/06/the-secrets-of-great-teamwork.

62 Haas and Mortensen, "The Secrets of Great Teamwork" (emphasis mine).

63 Or at least according to the author of the article: Tammy Erickson, "Meaning Is the New Money," *Harvard Business Review*, March 23, 2011, https://hbr.org/2011/03/challenging-our-deeply-held-as.

64 Shawn Achor et al., "9 Out of 10 People Are Willing to Earn Less Money to Do More-Meaningful Work," *Harvard Business Review*, November 6, 2018, https://hbr.org/2018/11/9-out-of-10-people-are-willing-to-earn-less-money-to-do-more-meaningful-work.

65 Sebastian Buck, "The Business Challenge of Our Time Is Creating Meaningful work," *Fast Company*, July 30, 2018, https://www.fastcompany.com/90208459/the-business-challenge-of-our-time-is-creating-meaningful-work.

66 Buck, "The Business Challenge of Our Time"; Jim Harter, "Dismal Employee Engagement Is a Sign of Global Mismanagement," Gallup (blog), accessed March 19, 2020, https://www.gallup.com/workplace/231668/dismal-employee-engagement-sign-global-mismanagement.aspx?g_source=link_WWWV9&g_medium=TOPIC&g_campaign=item_&g_content=Dismal%2520Employee%2520Engagement%2520Is%2520a%2520Sign%2520of%2520Global%2520Mismanagement.

67 Suzanne de Janasz and Maury Peiperl, "CEOs Need Mentors Too," *Harvard Business Review*, April 2015, https://hbr.org/2015/04/ceos-need-mentors-too.

68 De Janasz and Maury Peiperl, "CEOs Need Mentors Too."

69 De Janasz and Maury Peiperl, "CEOs Need Mentors Too."

70 De Janasz and Maury Peiperl, "CEOs Need Mentors Too."

71 Robert Puff, "Growth Mindset vs. Fixed Mindset," *Psychology Today*, September 19, 2017, https://www.psychologytoday.com/us/blog/meditation-modern-life/201709/growth-mindset-vs-fixed-mindset.

72 "Heuristics," *Psychology Today*, accessed April 8, 2020. https://www.psychologytoday.com/us/basics/heuristics.

73 "Heuristics," *American Psychological Association*, November 9, 2017, https://www.apa.org/pubs/highlights/peeps/issue-105.

74 Randy Pennington, "A Piece of Colored Ribbon," *Huffington Post*, December 11, 2016, https://www.huffpost.com/entry/a-piece-of-colored-ribbon_b_13440926.

75 John Amodeo, "Why We Like Being Appreciated," *Psychology Today*, April 23, 2016, https://www.psychologytoday.com/us/blog/intimacy-path-toward-spirituality/201604/why-we-being-appreciated.

76 "What Is Self-Esteem? A Psychologist Explains (2020 Update)," *Positive Psychology*, March 21, 2020, https://positivepsychology.com/self-esteem/.

77 "Counterproductive Work Behavior: CWB-I—IresearchNet," *Psychology*, January 29, 2016, http://psychology.iresearchnet.com/industrial-organizational-psychology/organizational-behavior/counterproductive-work-behavior-cwb-i/.

78 Michael W. Boye, and Amy R. Wasserman, "Predicting Counter-productivity among Drug Store Applicants," *Journal of Business and Psychology* 10, no. 3 (1996): 337–49, https://doi.org/10.1007/bf02249607.

79 Georgia Frances King, "How the Relationship Theory of 'Love Languages' Can Help Your Workplace Relationships, Too," *Quartz*, August 16, 2017, https://qz.com/1053563/love-languages-in-the-workplace-how-the-relationship-theory-can-help-your-office-relationships-too/.

80 Alfie Kohn, "Why Incentive Plans Cannot Work," *Harvard Business Review*, September/October 1993, https://hbr.org/1993/09/why-incentive-plans-cannot-work?referral=03759&cm_vc=rr_item_page. bottom.

81 Kohn, "Why Incentive Plans Cannot Work."

82 Bennett Stewart et al., "Rethinking Rewards," *Harvard Business Review*, November/December 1993, https://hbr.org/1993/11/rethinking-rewards.

83 Bennett Stewart et al., "Rethinking Rewards."

84 Bennett Stewart et al., "Rethinking Rewards."

85 Jurgen Appelo, "Better Ways to Reward Employees: Six Rules for Incentives," *Forbes*, September 25, 2015, https://www.forbes.com/sites/jurgenappelo/2015/09/25/better-ways-to-reward-employees-6-rules-for-incentives/#1f2c14bf3b50.

86 Adam Kearney, "We Digitized Google's Peer Recognition," *Medium*, May 2, 2016, https://medium.com/@K3ARN3Y/how-google-does-peer-recognition-188446e329dd.

87 Kearney, "We Digitized Google's Peer Recognition."

88   For this discussion of the five love languages in a workplace setting, I rely on the following: Ashley Faus, "The 5 Love Languages: Office Edition," *Muse*, accessed April 12, 2020, https://www.themuse.com/advice/the-5-love-languages-office-edition.

89   CJ McClanahan, "The Platinum Rule: Why It's Time to Forget How You Want to Be Treated," *Forbes*, March 23, 2020, https://www.forbes.com/sites/forbescoachescouncil/2020/03/23/the-platinum-rule-why-its-time-to-forget-how-you-want-to-be-treated/#d20c4d458ee4.

90   McClanahan, "The Platinum Rule."

91   Travis Bradberry, "8 Mistakes That Make Good Employees Leave," *Inc.*, accessed April 12, 2020, https://www.inc.com/travis-bradberry/8-mistakes-that-make-good-employees-leave.html.

92   Michael E. Kibler, "Prevent Your Star Performers from Losing Passion for Their Work," *Harvard Business Review*, January 14, 2015, https://hbr.org/2015/01/prevent-your-star-performers-from-losing-passion-in-their-work.

93   Kibler, "Prevent Your Star Performers."

94   For this profile on China, I rely on Martin Reeves et al., "How Chinese Companies Have Responded to Coronavirus," *Harvard Business Review*, March 10, 2020, https://hbr.org/2020/03/how-chinese-companies-have-responded-to-coronavirus.

95   Martin Reeves et al., "How Chinese Companies Have Responded."

96   Martin Reeves et al., "How Chinese Companies Have Responded."

97   Dan Sullivan, *The 4 C's Formula: Your Building Blocks of Growth; Commitment, Courage, Capability, and Confidence* (Toronto, 2015), 8.

98   Sullivan, *The 4 C's Formula*, 8.

99 Sullivan, *The 4 C's Formula*, 8.

100 Sullivan, *The 4 C's Formula*, 10

101 Sullivan, *The 4 C's Formula*, 10

102 Sullivan, *The 4 C's Formula*, 10

103 Sullivan, *The 4 C's Formula*, 11 passim.

104 Sullivan, *The 4 C's Formula*, 43.

105 "Confident Leaders Inspire Creativity," *Association for Psychological Science*, February 25, 2016, https://www.psychologicalscience.org/news/minds-business/confident-leaders-inspire-creativity.html.

106 Clifford N. Lazarus, "Do You Confuse People's 'States' with Their 'Traits?" *Psychology Today*, October 20, 2017, https://www.psychologytoday.com/us/blog/think-well/201710/do-you-confuse-peoples-states-their-traits.

107 Icek Ajzen, "From Intentions to Actions: A Theory of Planned Behavior," *Action Control* (1985): 11–39, https://doi.org/10.1007/978-3-642-69746-3_2.

108 "Human Relations: Self-Esteem and Self-Confidence Effects," *Human Relations*, accessed April 2, 2020, https://saylordotorg.github.io/text_human-relations/s05-04-human-relations-self-esteem-an.html.

109 Walter Isaacson, "The Real Leadership Lessons of Steve Jobs," *Harvard Business Review*, April 2012, https://hbr.org/2012/04/the-real-leadership-lessons-of-steve-jobs.

110 Isaacson, "The Real Leadership Lessons."

111 Rick Tetzeli, "The Evolution of Steve Jobs," *Fast Company*, March 16, 2015, https://www.fastcompany.com/3042433/the-real-legacy-of-steve-jobs.

112 Tetzeli, "The Evolution of Steve Jobs."

113 Yukari Iwatani Kane, "The Job After Steve Jobs: Tim Cook and Apple," *Wall Street Journal*, February 28, 2014, https://www.wsj.com/articles/the-job-after-steve-jobs-tim-cook-and-apple-1393637952.

114 Robert Frank, "Billionaire Sara Blakely says secret to success is failure," *CNBC*, October 16, 2013, https://www.cnbc.com/2013/10/16/billionaire-sara-blakely-says-secret-to-success-is-failure.html.

115 Frank, "Billionaire Sara Blakely."

116 Teri Evans, "Sara Blakely on Resilience," *Entrepreneur*, March 21, 2011, https://www.entrepreneur.com/article/219367.

117 Frank, "Billionaire Sara Blakely."

118 Evans, "Sara Blakely on Resilience."

119 Evans, "Sara Blakely on Resilience."

120 Frank, "Billionaire Sara Blakely."

121 Evans, "Sara Blakely on Resilience."

122 Frank, "Billionaire Sara Blakely."

123 Frank, "Billionaire Sara Blakely."

124 Frank, "Billionaire Sara Blakely."

125 For this discussion, I am indebted to Rick Woolsworth, "Great Mentors Focus on the Whole Person, Not Just Their Career," *Harvard Business Review*, August 9, 2019, https://hbr.org/2019/08/great-mentors-focus-on-the-whole-person-not-just-their-career.

126 Jennifer Moss, "Burnout Is about Your Workplace, Not Your People," *Harvard Business Review*, December 11, 2019, https://hbr.org/2019/12/burnout-is-about-your-workplace-not-your-people?utm_medium=social&utm_campaign=hbr&utm_source=linkedin.

127 Moss, "Burnout Is about Your Workplace."